THE COMPLETE
NO POINT
WEIGHT LOSS
COOKBOOK

*Satisfying Recipes That Keep You Full and Slim
Without Counting Calories with 30-Day Meal Plan*

Dr. Rachel C. Jenkins

Copyright

Contents

Dedication

This book is dedicated to all the incredible individuals who are on a journey to a healthier, happier self. To those who believe in the power of nourishing their bodies while enjoying every bite. This is for you, the person who refuses to compromise on flavor, even while working towards your weight loss goals.

May these recipes bring you satisfaction, joy, and the confidence that comes with knowing you are taking care of yourself in the best possible way. Here's to your success, one delicious meal at a time.

Acknowledgements

Creating the No-Point Weight Loss Cookbook has been a rewarding journey, and there are many people who have supported and inspired me along the way.

First and foremost, I want to express my deepest gratitude to my readers. Your dedication to living a healthier lifestyle and your enthusiasm for finding delicious, satisfying meals have been the driving force behind this book. It is for you that I've poured my heart into every recipe, and I hope this cookbook becomes a valuable resource on your journey to wellness.

I'd like to thank my family and friends for their unwavering support and encouragement. Your taste testing, honest feedback, and endless patience have been invaluable. I'm especially grateful for your willingness to try countless recipe variations until we found the perfect balance of flavor and health.

A special thanks to the talented chefs, nutritionists, and wellness experts who have shared their knowledge and expertise with me over the years. Your insights have greatly influenced the creation of this book, and your passion for healthy living continues to inspire me.

Finally, I want to acknowledge the incredible community of fellow health enthusiasts and food lovers. Your shared stories, tips, and experiences have not only shaped this cookbook but have also reminded me of the power of community in achieving our goals together.

To everyone who has contributed to this project, whether through direct involvement or simply by offering a kind word of encouragement, thank you. This cookbook would not have been possible without you, and I am forever grateful for your support.

With gratitude,

Rachel Jenkins

Introduction

Welcome to the No-Point Weight Loss Cookbook, your ultimate guide to delicious, satisfying meals that support your weight loss journey without the need for tedious tracking or portion control. This cookbook is designed for anyone looking to lose weight in a sustainable, enjoyable way, using recipes made entirely from zero-point foods.

What Are No-Point Foods?

No-point foods are those that you can eat freely while on the Weight Watchers program, thanks to their low-calorie, nutrient-dense profiles. These foods include a wide variety of fruits, vegetables, lean proteins, and other healthy ingredients that naturally promote satiety and provide essential nutrients. By focusing on these foods, you can create meals that are not only healthy and filling but also flexible enough to fit into your busy lifestyle.

Why Choose No-Point Recipes?

The beauty of no-point recipes lies in their simplicity and flexibility. These meals are built around foods that are naturally low in calories but high in nutrients, meaning you can enjoy generous portions without the need for constant monitoring or tracking. This approach takes the stress out of meal planning and helps you develop a healthier relationship with food, where you can eat until you're satisfied, not just until you've reached a certain point limit.

What's Inside?

In this cookbook, you'll find a diverse collection of breakfast, lunch, dinner, snack, and dessert recipes that are all crafted from zero-point foods. Each recipe is designed to be easy to prepare, using ingredients that are both accessible and affordable. Whether you're looking for a quick weekday breakfast or a hearty dinner to share with family, these recipes have you covered.

Balanced and Satisfying Meals

The recipes in this book aren't just about losing weight—they're about enjoying your food and feeling satisfied after every meal. We've focused on creating dishes that are not only nutritious but also bursting with flavor, so you never feel deprived. From hearty vegetable soups to refreshing fruit salads, each meal is crafted to keep you full, energized, and on track with your weight loss goals.

A Sustainable Approach to Weight Loss

Sustainable weight loss is about finding a balance that works for you long-term. By incorporating these no-point recipes into your routine, you're not just losing weight; you're building a lifestyle that supports your overall health and well-being. This cookbook is here to help you make that transition smoother, offering meals that you can enjoy day after day, with no need for strict dieting or calorie counting.

So grab your apron, and let's get cooking! With the No-Point Weight Loss Cookbook, you're on your way to a healthier, happier you—one delicious meal at a time.

How This Cookbook Can Help You

This No-Point Weight Loss Cookbook is more than just a collection of recipes—it's a practical tool designed to support you on your journey to a healthier, happier you. Here's how this cookbook can help you achieve your weight loss goals while enjoying the process:

1. Simplifies Your Weight Loss Journey

One of the biggest challenges in losing weight is navigating what to eat and how much to eat. This cookbook takes the guesswork out of meal planning by providing you with a variety of satisfying, zero-point recipes that are both nutritious and delicious. With these recipes, you can enjoy full, balanced meals without the stress of counting calories or tracking every bite.

2. Encourages Healthy Eating Habits

By focusing on zero-point foods—those that are naturally low in calories and rich in nutrients—this cookbook helps you develop healthier eating habits. The recipes emphasize whole, unprocessed foods that fuel your body and keep you full, making it easier to stick to your weight loss plan. Over time, these habits can lead to sustainable weight loss and improved overall health.

3. Provides Variety and Flexibility

One of the keys to sticking with any eating plan is variety, and this cookbook delivers just that. With a wide range of breakfast, lunch, dinner, snack, and dessert recipes, you'll never get bored with your meals. The cookbook is also designed to be flexible, allowing you to mix and match recipes to suit your tastes and lifestyle. Whether you're cooking for yourself, your family, or guests, you'll find recipes that everyone will love.

4. Makes Meal Planning Easy

Planning meals can be time-consuming, but with the included 30-day meal plan, you have a ready-made guide to help you stay on track. The meal plan is thoughtfully designed to ensure you get a balanced variety of meals each week, taking the stress out of what to cook next. Plus, with pre-made grocery shopping lists, you can easily stock your kitchen with everything you need.

5. Supports Sustainable Weight Loss

The recipes in this cookbook are not just about losing weight—they're about doing it in a way that is sustainable and enjoyable. By focusing on foods that are satisfying and nutritious, you're more likely to stick with your plan and avoid the pitfalls of fad diets that often lead to yo-yo dieting. This cookbook helps you build a healthy relationship with food, making it easier to maintain your weight loss over the long term.

6. Boosts Your Confidence and Motivation

As you follow the recipes and see the results—whether it's shedding pounds, feeling more energized, or simply enjoying your meals more—you'll likely find your confidence and motivation growing. This positive feedback loop can help keep you committed to your goals and make the weight loss journey feel more rewarding.

7. Promotes Enjoyment of Food

Eating well doesn't have to mean giving up the flavors and foods you love. This cookbook shows you that healthy, low-point meals can be just as tasty and satisfying as any other dish. By enjoying what you eat, you're more likely to stay committed to your weight loss plan and make lasting changes to your diet.

8. Empowers You to Take Control

With the tools and knowledge provided in this cookbook, you're empowered to take control of your eating habits and weight loss journey. The easy-to-follow recipes and practical advice make it simple to integrate healthy eating into your daily routine, putting you in charge of your health and well-being

Understanding No Point Weight Loss Recipes

Understanding no-point weight loss recipes is key to effectively following a weight loss program like Weight Watchers that emphasizes healthy eating without the need for strict calorie counting or portion control. Here's what you need to know about no-point recipes and how they work:

1. What Are No-Point Recipes?

Definition: No-point recipes are meals or snacks made entirely from foods that are considered "zero points" in the Weight Watchers program. These foods have been identified as low-calorie, nutrient-dense options that you can eat freely without tracking points.

Purpose: The goal of no-point recipes is to provide satisfying, nutritious meals that support weight loss without the need for meticulous tracking or portion control. This approach encourages you to eat more whole, unprocessed foods while still enjoying a variety of flavors and textures.

2. Key Components of No-Point Recipes:

Lean Proteins: Many no-point recipes include lean proteins like chicken breast, turkey, fish, eggs, tofu, and beans. These proteins are filling and help build and repair muscle, which is important during weight loss.

Non-Starchy Vegetables: Vegetables like spinach, broccoli, bell peppers, zucchini, and carrots are often the base of no-point recipes. They are low in calories, high in fiber, and packed with vitamins and minerals.

Fruits: Fresh fruits like berries, apples, oranges, and melons are common in no-point recipes, especially for breakfasts, snacks, and desserts. They add natural sweetness and essential nutrients.

Healthy Fats (in moderation): While many fats are not zero points, some healthy fats like those from fish (e.g., salmon), and small amounts of avocado or nuts may be included in recipes with careful consideration.

3. Why They Work for Weight Loss:

Satiety: No-point recipes focus on foods that naturally help you feel full due to their high fiber, water, and protein content. This helps control hunger and reduces the likelihood of overeating.

Nutrient Density: These recipes are designed to provide a lot of nutrients for relatively few calories. This means you can eat a larger volume of food while still losing weight, as you are getting the nutrients your body needs without excess energy intake.

Simplicity: By focusing on no-point foods, you reduce the need to constantly track what you eat. This simplifies the process of sticking to a weight loss plan and makes it easier to maintain over time.

4. Building a Balanced No-Point Meal:

Protein: Start with a lean protein source, such as grilled chicken, fish, tofu, or beans. Protein is crucial for muscle maintenance and helps keep you full.

Vegetables: Add a variety of non-starchy vegetables. These can be steamed, roasted, sautéed, or eaten raw in salads. Vegetables add bulk to your meal, helping you feel full and satisfied.

Fruits: Incorporate a piece of fruit or a small fruit salad as a side dish or dessert. Fruits provide natural sweetness and important vitamins.

Flavorings: Use herbs, spices, lemon juice, vinegar, and other low- or zero-calorie flavorings to enhance the taste without adding points. For example, garlic, ginger, fresh herbs, and mustard are all zero points and add depth to your dishes.

5. Examples of No-Point Recipes:

Breakfast: An egg white omelet with bell peppers, onions, and spinach, served with a side of fresh fruit.

Lunch: A grilled chicken salad with mixed greens, cherry tomatoes, cucumbers, and a balsamic vinegar dressing.

Dinner: Baked cod with steamed broccoli and a squeeze of lemon, accompanied by roasted carrots and Brussels sprouts.

Snacks: Cucumber slices topped with tuna salad made with Greek yogurt and a sprinkle of fresh herbs.

Dessert: A fresh fruit salad with mixed berries, kiwi, and a dash of cinnamon.

6. Flexibility and Variety:

Variety: No-point recipes offer a wide variety of flavors and cuisines, from hearty soups and stews to light salads and grilled dishes. This variety helps prevent diet fatigue and keeps your meals interesting.

Customization: You can customize no-point recipes to suit your tastes and dietary needs. For example, you can swap out vegetables or proteins based on what you have on hand or what you prefer.

7. Considerations:

Portion Control: While no-point foods can be eaten freely, it's still important to listen to your body's hunger and fullness cues. Eating large amounts of even zero-point foods can slow weight loss if it leads to a calorie surplus.

Balance: While no-point recipes are great for meals, it's important to ensure your overall diet is balanced. Incorporate healthy fats and whole grains in moderation, even if they aren't zero points, to ensure you're getting a well-rounded diet.

8. Sustainability:

No-point recipes are designed to be part of a sustainable lifestyle. By focusing on whole foods that you can eat without tracking, you create habits that are easier to maintain long-term, reducing the likelihood of regaining lost weight.

In summary, no-point weight loss recipes are an effective way to enjoy nutritious, satisfying meals without the stress of counting calories or points. They focus on foods that naturally support weight loss through their nutrient density and satiety, making them an excellent tool for sustainable weight management.

How No Point Foods Are Chosen

Zero-point foods are selected based on their nutritional profile, including their ability to support weight loss and healthy eating without contributing to excessive calorie intake. The idea behind zero-point foods is that they are nutritious, low in calories, and satisfying, allowing you to eat them freely without worrying about tracking or portion control. Here's how these foods are typically chosen:

1. Nutrient Density:

Zero-point foods are rich in essential nutrients like vitamins, minerals, and fiber while being low in calories. These foods provide a lot of nutritional value for relatively few calories, helping you meet your daily nutrient needs without overconsuming calories.

2. Low Energy Density:

Foods that are low in energy density (calories per gram) tend to fill you up with fewer calories. This is why many fruits, vegetables, and lean proteins are zero points—they take up space in your stomach and help you feel full without adding a lot of calories.

3. Natural Satiety:

Foods that are high in protein, fiber, and water content naturally promote a feeling of fullness and satisfaction. This reduces the likelihood of overeating. For example, eggs, chicken breast, and non-starchy vegetables are all filling and low in calories, making them good candidates for zero-point foods.

4. Minimal Processing:

Zero-point foods are usually whole or minimally processed. This means they are closer to their natural state, with little to no added sugars, fats, or preservatives. This helps ensure that these foods are healthier and more supportive of weight loss goals.

5. Health Benefits:

The foods chosen often have additional health benefits, such as reducing the risk of chronic diseases, improving digestion, and supporting overall wellness. For example, fruits and vegetables are rich in antioxidants, vitamins, and minerals that contribute to good health.

6. Low in Added Sugars and Fats:

Foods that are naturally low in added sugars and unhealthy fats are prioritized. This is why many lean proteins, non-starchy vegetables, and plain, unsweetened dairy products qualify as zero points.

7. Encouragement of Healthy Habits:

The selection of zero-point foods is designed to encourage the consumption of more wholesome, nutritious foods. This helps develop and maintain healthy eating habits that can be sustained over the long term.

8. Support for Weight Loss:

Since these foods are low in calories and high in nutrients, they support weight loss by allowing you to eat satisfying portions without exceeding your calorie needs. This reduces the reliance on portion control and tracking, making weight loss more manageable.

Examples of Zero-Point Food Categories:

Fruits: Naturally sweet and low in calories, fruits like berries, apples, and oranges are zero points because they are packed with fiber, vitamins, and antioxidants.

Vegetables: Non-starchy vegetables like spinach, broccoli, and bell peppers are nutrient-dense, low-calorie foods that you can eat in abundance.

Lean Proteins: Foods like skinless chicken breast, turkey breast, eggs, and seafood are high in protein, which helps with satiety and muscle maintenance.

Non-Fat Dairy: Options like fat-free plain Greek yogurt and cottage cheese provide protein and calcium without added sugars or fats.

Legumes: Beans, lentils, and peas are high in fiber and protein, making them filling and nutritious while being low in calories.

Flexibility Across Plans:

Different versions of the Weight Watchers program might have slightly varying lists of zero-point foods, depending on the plan's focus. For instance, some plans might include fat-free yogurt or corn as zero points, while others may not. The idea is to tailor the zero-point foods to the individual's needs and preferences, promoting adherence to the plan.

zero-point foods are chosen for their ability to contribute positively to a healthy diet while being low enough in calories to support weight loss without the need for strict tracking or portion control. They are carefully selected to be filling, nutritious, and easy to incorporate into daily meals.

Characteristics of Zero Point Foods:

Low-Calorie Density: These foods generally have a high water and fiber content, which makes them filling without being high in calories.

Nutrient-Rich: They are rich in vitamins, minerals, and other essential nutrients, supporting overall health while promoting weight loss.

Satiating: Due to their fiber and protein content, they tend to keep you fuller for longer, reducing the temptation to snack on higher-calorie foods.

Categories of Zero Point Foods:

Fruits: Most fruits are zero points, except for those with added sugar or dried fruits. Examples include apples, bananas, berries, grapes, and oranges.

Vegetables: Non-starchy vegetables are typically zero points. This includes leafy greens, tomatoes, cucumbers, broccoli, and cauliflower.

Lean Proteins: Certain lean proteins like skinless chicken breast, turkey breast, and fish (including salmon, tilapia, and shellfish) are zero points.

Legumes and Beans: Beans, lentils, and peas are included in the zero-point list, providing a good source of plant-based protein and fiber.

Non-Fat Dairy and Eggs: Eggs and non-fat Greek yogurt are also zero points, making them versatile options for meals and snacks.

Benefits of Zero Point Foods

1. Flexibility in Dieting:

The concept of Zero Point foods allows you to eat without feeling restricted, helping to create a sustainable and enjoyable diet.

They enable more flexibility in using your daily SmartPoints on other foods, such as occasional treats or higher-point meals.

2. Encourages Healthy Eating Habits:

By focusing on Zero Point foods, you naturally gravitate towards more nutritious, whole foods.

These foods promote a balanced diet that's rich in fruits, vegetables, lean proteins, and whole grains.

3. Simplified Meal Planning:

Zero Point foods simplify meal planning and tracking, making it easier to stay within your daily point allowance without meticulous tracking.

Incorporating Zero Point Foods into Your Diet

1. Start with Breakfast:

Incorporate eggs, non-fat Greek yogurt, and fruits like berries or bananas into your morning routine. This sets the tone for a healthy day.

2. Bulk Up Meals with Vegetables:

Add a variety of non-starchy vegetables to your lunch and dinner. This not only increases the volume of your meals but also boosts their nutritional content.

3. Snack Wisely:

Use Zero Point fruits and vegetables as snacks throughout the day. They are satisfying and prevent you from reaching for higher-point options.

4. Smart Pairing:

Pair Zero Point foods with other low-point items to create satisfying, complete meals. For example, combine a piece of lean chicken breast with a side of sautéed spinach and roasted sweet potatoes.

5. Keep it Balanced:

While Zero Point foods are free to consume, it's essential to maintain a balanced diet and not overeat even these healthy options. Focus on portion control and variety.

Tips for Success

Stay Hydrated: Drinking water is crucial for overall health and weight loss. Consider infusing your water with Zero Point fruits like lemon or berries for added flavor.

Plan Ahead: Use Zero Point foods as the foundation of your meal planning. This approach can simplify your diet and help you stay on track.

Experiment with Recipes: Try new ways to prepare Zero Point foods to keep your meals exciting. Whether it's roasting vegetables, making a fresh fruit salad, or grilling lean meats, variety is key.

By focusing on Zero Point foods, you can create a diet that supports weight loss while allowing for flexibility and enjoyment in your meals. The goal is to build sustainable eating habits that help you achieve and maintain a healthy weight long-term.

Veggie-Packed Scrambled Eggs with Spinach, Mushrooms, and Tomatoes

This Veggie-Packed Scrambled Eggs recipe is a perfect zero-point breakfast option that is both filling and nutritious. It combines the protein power of eggs with the fiber-rich goodness of spinach, mushrooms, and tomatoes, all of which are zero-point foods according to Weight Watchers guidelines. This simple yet satisfying meal will keep you energized and help you stay on track with your weight loss goals.

Prep time: 5 minutes | Cooking time: 10 minutes | Servings: 1 (adjust as needed)

Ingredients (0 points):

- 2 large eggs
- 1/2 cup fresh spinach, chopped
- 1/4 cup mushrooms, sliced
- 1/4 cup cherry tomatoes, halved
- 1 clove garlic, minced
- Salt and pepper to taste
- Cooking spray or a small amount of water for sautéing

Step-by-Step Directions:

1. Prep Your Ingredients (0 points): I start by washing and chopping the spinach, slicing the mushrooms, and halving the cherry tomatoes. I also mince the garlic to add an extra layer of flavor to my scrambled eggs.
2. Sauté the Vegetables: I spray a non-stick pan lightly with cooking spray (or use a tiny bit of water) and heat it over medium heat. I then add the minced garlic and cook it for about 30 seconds until it's fragrant, being careful not to let it burn. Next, I toss in the mushrooms and cook them for 2-3 minutes until they start to soften. After that, I add the spinach and cherry tomatoes and cook for another 2 minutes until the spinach is wilted and the tomatoes are slightly softened.
3. Scramble the Eggs: While the vegetables are cooking, I crack the eggs into a small bowl and beat them lightly with a fork. Once the vegetables are ready, I pour the beaten eggs over the veggie mixture in the pan. I gently stir everything together, allowing the eggs to cook and scramble around the vegetables. This usually takes about 2-3 minutes, depending on how I like my eggs cooked.
4. Season and Serve: I season the scrambled eggs with a pinch of salt and pepper to taste, then transfer them to a plate. It's a simple yet hearty breakfast that I can enjoy guilt-free.

Tips:

1. Add Extra Veggies: If I want to change things up, I sometimes add other zero-point veggies like bell peppers, onions, or zucchini.
2. Bulk Cooking: I can easily double or triple this recipe if I'm cooking for more people or if I want to meal prep for the week.
3. Herbs: Fresh herbs like parsley or chives can add extra flavor without adding points.

Nutritional Information:

- Calories: 140, Protein: 12g, Fat: 9g, Carbohydrates: 4g, Fiber: 1.5g, Sugar: 2g, Points: 0

Serving Suggestions:

1. Add a Side: Sometimes I like to serve this dish with a side of fresh fruit like berries or a small serving of non-fat Greek yogurt for extra protein.
2. Whole Wheat Toast (Optional): If I'm looking to add some carbs to my meal, I might include a slice of whole wheat toast, but I'll make sure to count the points.

Greek Yogurt with Mixed Berries and a Sprinkle of Cinnamon

This recipe is a delicious, quick, and easy breakfast that's perfect for those busy mornings when you need something nutritious and satisfying. Greek yogurt provides a great source of protein, while the mixed berries add natural sweetness and plenty of fiber. A sprinkle of cinnamon ties it all together, adding warmth and flavor without any extra points. This recipe fits perfectly into the Zero Point Weight Loss program, helping me stay on track with my weight loss goals.

Prep time: 5 minutes | Cooking time: None | Servings: 1 (adjust as needed)

Ingredients (0 points):

- 1 cup non-fat plain Greek yogurt
- 1/2 cup fresh mixed berries (such as strawberries, blueberries, and raspberries)
- 1/4 teaspoon ground cinnamon

Step-by-Step Directions:

1. Prepare the Ingredients (0 points): I start by gathering my Ingredients (0 points): non-fat Greek yogurt, fresh mixed berries, and ground cinnamon. I make sure the berries are washed and ready to go.
2. Assemble the Dish: In a bowl, I spoon out 1 cup of non-fat plain Greek yogurt. I then top it with 1/2 cup of the fresh mixed berries. I like to mix different berries for a variety of flavors and textures.
3. I finish by sprinkling 1/4 teaspoon of ground cinnamon over the top. This adds a lovely aroma and a touch of spice that complements the sweetness of the berries.
4. Serve: My Greek yogurt with mixed berries and cinnamon is ready to eat. I simply grab a spoon and enjoy!

Tips:

1. Berry Variations: I sometimes swap out the berries depending on what's in season or what I have on hand. Blackberries and cherries work well too.
2. Extra Flavor: If I'm in the mood for a little extra flavor, I might add a drop or two of vanilla extract to the yogurt before adding the berries.
3. Texture: For a bit of crunch, I can add a small sprinkle of chopped nuts or seeds, but I'll need to account for the points if I do.

Nutritional Information:

- Calories: 120, Protein: 20g, Fat: 0g, Carbohydrates: 14g, Fiber: 3g, Sugar: 10g, Points: 0

Serving Suggestions:

1. Optional Add-Ons: If I'm looking to make this breakfast a bit more filling, I might add a small portion of whole grain cereal or oats on top, but I'll be sure to calculate the additional points.
2. On-the-Go: If I'm in a hurry, I can layer the ingredients in a portable container and take it with me. It's a great option for a quick, healthy breakfast on the go.

Egg White Omelet with Bell Peppers, Onions, and Fresh Herbs

This Egg White Omelet is a light, protein-packed breakfast that's perfect for starting my day on the right foot. By using just egg whites, I keep the dish low in calories while still getting plenty of protein. The addition of bell peppers, onions, and fresh herbs adds flavor, color, and essential nutrients without any extra points. This recipe is simple, satisfying, and fits perfectly into the Zero Point Weight Loss program.

Prep time: 5 minutes | Cooking time: 10 minutes | Servings: 1 (adjust as needed)

Ingredients (0 points):

- 4 large egg whites
- 1/4 cup bell peppers, diced (any color)
- 1/4 cup onions, diced (0 points)
- 1 tablespoon fresh parsley or chives, chopped
- Salt and pepper to taste
- Cooking spray or a small amount of water for sautéing

Step-by-Step Directions:

1. Prep the Vegetables: I start by dicing the bell peppers and onions. I also chop the fresh herbs, which I'll add at the end for a burst of flavor.
2. Cook the Vegetables: In a non-stick pan, I lightly spray cooking spray (or use a little water) and heat it over medium heat. I add the diced onions and bell peppers to the pan and sauté them for about 3-4 minutes until they're soft and slightly caramelized.
3. Prepare the Egg Whites: While the vegetables are cooking, I separate the egg whites from the yolks and whisk the egg whites in a small bowl until they're slightly frothy. This helps create a light, fluffy omelet.
4. Cook the Omelet: Once the vegetables are cooked, I reduce the heat to low and pour the egg whites over the sautéed vegetables in the pan. I let the mixture cook for about 3-4 minutes, gently lifting the edges with a spatula to allow the uncooked egg whites to flow underneath.When the egg whites are mostly set but still a little soft on top, I sprinkle the fresh herbs over the omelet.
5. Fold and Serve: I carefully fold the omelet in half and let it cook for another minute until fully set. Then, I slide it onto a plate and season with a pinch of salt and pepper to taste.

Tips:

1. Add More Veggies: If I want to bulk up my omelet, I might add other zero-point veggies like spinach, tomatoes, or mushrooms.
2. Cheese (Optional): If I'm craving a little more richness, I could add a small amount of low-fat cheese, but I'll need to account for the additional points.
3. Avoid Overcooking: To keep the omelet tender and avoid a rubbery texture, I make sure not to overcook the egg whites.

Nutritional Information:

- Calories: 60, Protein: 12g, Fat: 0g, Carbohydrates: 4g, Fiber: 1g, Sugar: 2g, Points: 0

Serving Suggestions:

1. Add a Side: I often serve this omelet with a side of fresh fruit or a small mixed green salad for a complete breakfast.
2. Whole Grain Toast (Optional): If I'm looking for something a bit heartier, I might add a slice of whole grain toast, but I'll make sure to count the points.

Spiced Apple and Oatmeal Breakfast Bowl (using unsweetened applesauce and spices)

This Spiced Apple and Oatmeal Breakfast Bowl is a warm, comforting start to my day, perfect for those mornings when I want something filling yet healthy. The combination of oatmeal, unsweetened applesauce, and warm spices like cinnamon and nutmeg creates a flavorful and satisfying dish that fits seamlessly into the Zero Point Weight Loss program. It's not only delicious but also nutritious, providing fiber and natural sweetness without any added sugars or points.

Prep time: 5 minutes | Cooking time: 10 minutes | Servings: 2

Ingredients (0 points):

- 1 cup old-fashioned oats
- 2 cups water
- 1/2 cup unsweetened applesauce
- 1 medium apple, peeled, cored, and diced
- 1 teaspoon ground cinnamon
- 1/4 teaspoon ground nutmeg
- 1/4 teaspoon vanilla extract
- Pinch of salt (optional,

Step-by-Step Directions:

1. Cook the Oats: I start by bringing 2 cups of water to a boil in a medium saucepan. Once boiling, I add 1 cup of old-fashioned oats and reduce the heat to medium-low.I let the oats cook for about 5 minutes, stirring occasionally, until they've absorbed most of the water and are soft.
2. Prepare the Apple Mixture: While the oats are cooking, I peel, core, and dice a medium apple. In a small bowl, I mix the diced apple with 1/2 cup of unsweetened applesauce, 1 teaspoon of ground cinnamon, 1/4 teaspoon of ground nutmeg, and 1/4 teaspoon of vanilla extract.
3. Combine and Heat: Once the oats are ready, I stir in the apple mixture. I continue to cook the oatmeal for another 3-5 minutes, stirring occasionally, until the apples are tender and the flavors have melded together.If I want a creamier texture, I can add a splash of water or unsweetened almond milk during this step.
4. Serve:I divide the Spiced Apple and Oatmeal mixture into two bowls. It's warm, flavorful, and ready to enjoy!

Tips:

1. Apple Varieties: I like to use sweet apples like Fuji or Gala for this recipe, but tart varieties like Granny Smith work well too if I prefer a tangier flavor.
2. Extra Spice: If I love spices, I can add a pinch of ground cloves or ginger for an extra kick.
3. Avoid Overcooking: I keep an eye on the oatmeal to prevent it from becoming too thick. If it does, I add a bit of water to loosen it up.

Nutritional Information:

- Calories: 180, Protein: 5g, Fat: 2g, Carbohydrates: 38g, Fiber: 6g, Sugar: 9g, Points: 0

Serving Suggestions:

1. Toppings: I sometimes top my oatmeal with additional fresh apple slices or a sprinkle of extra cinnamon for added texture and flavor.
2. Pairing: A side of plain non-fat Greek yogurt (0 points) pairs nicely with this oatmeal if I want to add some extra protein to my breakfast.

Cottage Cheese with Sliced Cucumbers and Cherry Tomatoes

This Cottage Cheese with Sliced Cucumbers and Cherry Tomatoes recipe is a refreshing and protein-packed breakfast that's both satisfying and incredibly easy to prepare. The creamy cottage cheese pairs perfectly with the crisp cucumbers and juicy cherry tomatoes, creating a balanced and delicious meal. This dish is perfect for when I need something quick and light that still fits into the Zero Point Weight Loss program.

Prep time: 5 minutes | Cooking time: None | Servings: 2

Ingredients (0 points):

- 1 cup fat-free cottage cheese
- 1/2 medium cucumber, thinly sliced
- 1/2 cup cherry tomatoes, halved
- 1 tablespoon fresh dill or parsley, chopped
- Salt and pepper to taste

Step-by-Step Directions:

1. Prepare the Ingredients (0 points): I begin by slicing the cucumber thinly and halving the cherry tomatoes. Fresh produce is key to making this dish both flavorful and satisfying.
2. Assemble the Dish: I divide the 1 cup of fat-free cottage cheese between two bowls. Then, I arrange the sliced cucumbers and halved cherry tomatoes on top of the cottage cheese in each bowl.
3. Season and Garnish: I sprinkle the chopped fresh dill or parsley over the top for added flavor and a touch of color. Finally, I season the dish with a pinch of salt and pepper to taste.
4. Serve: My Cottage Cheese with Sliced Cucumbers and Cherry Tomatoes is ready to eat. It's a simple, fresh, and satisfying breakfast that I can enjoy right away.

Tips:

1. Extra Flavor: Sometimes, I add a squeeze of fresh lemon juice over the top to brighten up the flavors even more.
2. Cucumber Variety: English cucumbers work well in this dish because they have fewer seeds and a milder flavor.
3. Fresh Herbs: If I'm out of dill or parsley, other fresh herbs like basil or chives also complement the dish nicely.

Nutritional Information:

- Calories: 80, Protein: 14g, Fat: 0g, Carbohydrates: 7g, Fiber: 1.5g, Sugar: 5g, Points: 0

Serving Suggestions:

1. Add a Side: For a more complete meal, I sometimes pair this dish with a slice of whole-grain toast (points counted separately) or a side of fresh fruit.
2. Make it a Snack: This recipe also works well as a quick snack during the day if I'm looking for something light but satisfying.

Baked Egg Cups with Zucchini, Red Bell Peppers, and Onions

These Baked Egg Cups with Zucchini, Red Bell Peppers, and Onions are a convenient and nutritious breakfast option that's perfect for busy mornings. They're packed with protein and vegetables, making them both satisfying and healthy. I can prepare them ahead of time, making it easy to stick to my Zero Point Weight Loss program without any hassle.

Prep time: 20 minutes | Cooking time: 20 minutes | Servings: 2 (makes 4 egg cups)

Ingredients (0 points):

- 4 large eggs
- 1/2 cup zucchini, diced
- 1/2 cup red bell pepper, diced
- 1/4 cup onion, finely chopped
- Cooking spray
- Salt and pepper to taste
- Optional: fresh herbs like parsley or chives, chopped

Step-by-Step Directions:

- Preheat the Oven: I preheat my oven to 375°F (190°C) and lightly spray a muffin tin with cooking spray to prevent sticking.
- Prepare the Vegetables: I start by dicing the zucchini and red bell pepper, and finely chopping the onion. I want the veggies to be small enough to fit nicely in the egg cups.
- Sauté the Vegetables: In a non-stick pan, I lightly spray cooking spray and sauté the diced zucchini, red bell pepper, and onion over medium heat for about 5 minutes, or until they are slightly softened. This step helps to bring out the flavors of the vegetables.
- Mix the Eggs: While the vegetables are cooking, I crack the eggs into a bowl and whisk them until they're well combined. I add a pinch of salt and pepper to season the eggs.
- Assemble the Egg Cups: I divide the sautéed vegetables evenly among the 4 muffin cups in the prepared tin. Then, I pour the beaten eggs over the vegetables, filling each cup almost to the top. If I'm using fresh herbs, I sprinkle them on top at this stage.
- Bake:I place the muffin tin in the preheated oven and bake for 15-20 minutes, or until the egg cups are set and slightly golden on top. I test for doneness by inserting a toothpick into the center of an egg cup; it should come out clean.
- Serve: Once baked, I allow the egg cups to cool for a couple of minutes before gently removing them from the tin. They're ready to enjoy warm, or I can save them for a quick grab-and-go breakfast.

Tips:

1. Add Extra Veggies: If I want to bulk up the egg cups, I can add other zero-point vegetables like spinach, mushrooms, or tomatoes.
2. Storage: These egg cups can be stored in the refrigerator for up to 3 days. I reheat them in the microwave for about 30 seconds before eating.

Nutritional Information:

- Calories: 120, Protein: 10g, Fat: 7g, Carbohydrates: 6g, Fiber: 1.5g, Sugar: 3g, Points: 0

Serving Suggestions:

1. Pair with Fruit: I like to serve these egg cups with a side of fresh fruit like berries or a sliced apple for a balanced meal.
2. Whole Grain Toast (Optional): If I'm looking for a heartier breakfast, I might add a slice of whole grain toast, but I'll make sure to account for the points.

Scrambled Tofu with Spinach, Bell Peppers, and Onions

This Scrambled Tofu with Spinach, Bell Peppers, and Onions is a flavorful, protein-rich breakfast that's perfect for a plant-based start to my day. Tofu provides a great source of plant-based protein, while the spinach, bell peppers, and onions add plenty of nutrients and color. This dish is satisfying, nutritious, and fits seamlessly into the Zero Point Weight Loss program.

Prep time: 10 minutes | Cooking time: 10 minutes | Servings: 2

Ingredients (0 points):

- 1 block (14 oz) firm tofu, drained and crumbled
- 1 cup fresh spinach, chopped
- 1/2 cup red bell pepper, diced
- 1/4 cup onion, finely chopped
- 1 clove garlic, minced
- 1/2 teaspoon turmeric
- 1/2 teaspoon cumin
- Salt and pepper to taste
- Cooking spray or a small amount of water for sautéing
- Optional: fresh parsley or chives, chopped

Step-by-Step Directions:

1. Prep the Tofu and Vegetables: I start by draining the tofu and then crumbling it into small pieces using my hands or a fork. I also chop the spinach, dice the bell pepper, finely chop the onion, and mince the garlic.
2. Cook the Vegetables: In a non-stick pan, I lightly spray cooking spray or add a small amount of water, then heat it over medium heat. I sauté the diced onion and bell pepper for about 3-4 minutes until they start to soften. I then add the minced garlic and cook for another minute, being careful not to let it burn.
3. Add the Tofu and Spices: Next, I add the crumbled tofu to the pan and stir everything together. I sprinkle in the turmeric and cumin, which not only add flavor but also give the tofu a nice color. I continue to cook for about 5-7 minutes, stirring occasionally, until the tofu is heated through and slightly browned.
4. Add the Spinach: I add the chopped spinach to the pan and stir it into the tofu mixture. The spinach will wilt quickly, usually within a minute or two. I then season the scramble with a pinch of salt and pepper to taste.
5. Serve: Once everything is well combined and cooked through, I divide the scrambled tofu between two plates. If I'm using fresh herbs, I sprinkle them over the top as a garnish.

Tips:

1. Extra Veggies: If I want to add more variety, I can include other zero-point vegetables like mushrooms, zucchini, or tomatoes.
2. Flavor Boost: A squeeze of fresh lemon juice or a dash of hot sauce can add a nice zing to the dish.
3. Storage: This dish keeps well in the fridge for up to 3 days. I reheat it in the microwave or on the stove for a quick meal.

Nutritional Information:

- Calories: 150, Protein: 15g, Fat: 8g, Carbohydrates: 8g, Fiber: 3g, Sugar: 2g, Points: 0

Serving Suggestions:

1. Add a Side: I sometimes serve this scramble with a side of fresh fruit like orange slices or berries for a balanced breakfast.
2. Wrap it Up: For a portable option, I can wrap the scramble in a large lettuce leaf or a low-point tortilla (points counted separately) for a breakfast wrap.

Berry Smoothie with Unsweetened Almond Milk and a Handful of Spinach

This Berry Smoothie with Unsweetened Almond Milk and Spinach is a refreshing, nutrient-packed breakfast that's perfect for busy mornings. It combines the natural sweetness of berries with the creamy texture of unsweetened almond milk and the nutritional benefits of spinach, all while keeping the points at zero. This smoothie is not only delicious but also loaded with vitamins, fiber, and antioxidants, making it a great way to kickstart my day while sticking to the Zero Point Weight Loss program.

Prep time: 5 minutes | Cooking time: None | Servings: 2

Ingredients (0 points):

- 1 cup mixed berries (such as strawberries, blueberries, raspberries)
- 1 cup unsweetened almond milk
- 1 handful fresh spinach (about 1 cup)
- 1/2 cup ice cubes (optional, for a thicker smoothie)
- 1/2 teaspoon vanilla extract (optional, for extra flavor)

Step-by-Step Directions:

- Prepare the Ingredients): I start by washing the berries and spinach thoroughly. I like to use a mix of berries for a balanced flavor, but I can adjust the ratio depending on what I have on hand.
- Blend the Smoothie: In a blender, I add 1 cup of mixed berries, 1 cup of unsweetened almond milk, and the handful of fresh spinach. If I want a thicker smoothie, I toss in the 1/2 cup of ice cubes. I blend the ingredients on high until the mixture is smooth and creamy. This usually takes about 30 seconds to 1 minute, depending on the power of my blender.
- Taste and Adjust: Once blended, I give the smoothie a quick taste. If I feel like it needs a little more flavor, I add the 1/2 teaspoon of vanilla extract and blend again briefly.
- Serve: I pour the smoothie into two glasses and enjoy it immediately. It's a refreshing, filling breakfast that takes just minutes to make.

Tips:

1. Frozen Berries: If fresh berries aren't available, I can use frozen berries instead. They also help thicken the smoothie, eliminating the need for ice.
2. Extra Greens: If I'm looking to boost the nutritional content even more, I can add a handful of kale along with the spinach.
3. Protein Boost: For a protein boost, I sometimes add a scoop of unsweetened protein powder, but I'll need to count any additional points.

Nutritional Information:

- Calories: 60, Protein: 2g, Fat: 2.5g, Carbohydrates: 10g, Fiber: 4g, Sugar: 5g, Points: 0

Serving Suggestions:

1. Toppings: Sometimes, I like to add a few extra berries or a sprinkle of chia seeds on top of my smoothie for added texture and nutrition (points for toppings may vary).
2. Pairing: This smoothie pairs well with a small slice of whole-grain toast if I need something more substantial, but I'll make sure to count the points.

Poached Eggs over a Bed of Sautéed Kale and Cherry Tomatoes

This recipe for Poached Eggs over a Bed of Sautéed Kale and Cherry Tomatoes is a nutritious and satisfying breakfast that's perfect for keeping me full and energized throughout the morning. The combination of tender poached eggs with the earthy flavor of kale and the sweetness of cherry tomatoes creates a balanced meal that fits perfectly within the Zero Point Weight Loss program. It's simple to make, delicious, and completely zero points.

Prep time: 5 minutes | Cooking time: 10 minutes | Servings: 2

Ingredients (0 points):

- 4 large eggs
- 2 cups kale, chopped
- 1 cup cherry tomatoes, halved
- 1 clove garlic, minced
- 1 teaspoon apple cider vinegar (for poaching)
- Salt and pepper to taste
- Cooking spray or a small amount of water for sautéing
- Optional: fresh herbs like parsley or chives, chopped

Step-by-Step Directions:

1. Prep the Ingredients: I start by chopping the kale and halving the cherry tomatoes. I also mince the garlic to add extra flavor to the sautéed vegetables.
2. Sauté the Kale and Tomatoes: In a non-stick pan, I lightly spray cooking spray or add a small amount of water, then heat it over medium heat. I add the minced garlic and cook it for about 30 seconds until fragrant. Next, I add the chopped kale and halved cherry tomatoes to the pan. I sauté them for 3-5 minutes until the kale is wilted and the tomatoes are slightly softened. I season the mixture with a pinch of salt and pepper.
3. Poach the Eggs: While the vegetables are cooking, I bring a small pot of water to a gentle simmer. I add 1 teaspoon of apple cider vinegar to the water, which helps the eggs hold their shape. I crack each egg into a small bowl, then gently slide the eggs one at a time into the simmering water. I poach the eggs for about 3-4 minutes until the whites are set, but the yolks are still runny. Using a slotted spoon, I carefully remove the eggs from the water and let them drain on a paper towel.
4. Assemble the Dish: I divide the sautéed kale and cherry tomatoes between two plates. I then place two poached eggs on top of each bed of vegetables. If I'm using fresh herbs, I sprinkle them over the top for a burst of color and flavor.
5. Serve: My Poached Eggs over a Bed of Sautéed Kale and Cherry Tomatoes is ready to enjoy. It's a light, satisfying breakfast that's perfect for any day of the week.

Tips:

- Egg Poaching: If I'm new to poaching eggs, I can use a fine mesh strainer to remove the excess egg whites before poaching. This helps create a more uniform shape.
- Add Extra Veggies: If I want to bulk up the dish, I can add other zero-point vegetables like mushrooms or bell peppers to the sautéed mixture.
- Avoid Overcooking: I keep a close eye on the eggs while poaching to ensure the yolks stay runny, which adds richness to the dish.

Nutritional Information:

- Calories: 150, Protein: 14g, Fat: 9g, Carbohydrates: 6g, Fiber: 3g, Sugar: 3g, Points: 0

Serving Suggestions:

1. Add a Side: I sometimes serve this dish with a slice of whole-grain toast (points counted separately) or a side of fresh fruit for a more complete meal.

Fresh Fruit Salad with Grapefruit, Kiwi, and Berries

This Fresh Fruit Salad with Grapefruit, Kiwi, and Berries is a light and refreshing breakfast that's bursting with natural sweetness and flavor. It's packed with vitamins, antioxidants, and fiber, making it a perfect way to start the day. The combination of tart grapefruit, juicy kiwi, and sweet berries creates a balanced and satisfying dish that fits seamlessly into the Zero Point Weight Loss program.

Prep time: 10 minutes | Cooking time: None | Servings: 2

Ingredients (0 points):

- 1 grapefruit, peeled and segmented
- 2 kiwis, peeled and sliced
- 1/2 cup strawberries, hulled and sliced
- 1/2 cup blueberries
- 1/2 cup raspberries
- 1 tablespoon fresh mint, chopped (optional)

Step-by-Step Directions:

1. Prepare the Fruit: I start by peeling the grapefruit and carefully segmenting it, removing any seeds. I then peel and slice the kiwis, and hull and slice the strawberries.
2. Assemble the Salad: In a large mixing bowl, I combine the grapefruit segments, sliced kiwis, strawberries, blueberries, and raspberries. I gently toss the fruit together to ensure even distribution.
3. Add Fresh Mint (Optional): If I'm using fresh mint, I chop it finely and sprinkle it over the fruit salad. The mint adds a refreshing flavor that complements the sweetness of the fruit.
4. Serve: I divide the fruit salad into two bowls, and it's ready to enjoy. It's a vibrant, healthy breakfast that's perfect for a quick and easy start to my day.

Tips:

1. Chill Before Serving: If I have time, I like to chill the fruit salad in the refrigerator for 10-15 minutes before serving. It's even more refreshing when served cold.
2. Citrus Juices: I can add a squeeze of fresh lemon or lime juice over the fruit to enhance the flavors and add a bit of zing.
3. Variety: This recipe is versatile, so I can easily swap in other zero-point fruits like mango, pineapple, or oranges depending on what I have on hand.

Nutritional Information:

- Calories: 80, Protein: 2g, Fat: 0g, Carbohydrates: 20g, Fiber: 6g, Sugar: 14g, Points: 0

Serving Suggestions:

1. Yogurt Pairing: Sometimes, I pair this fruit salad with a dollop of plain non-fat Greek yogurt (0 points) for added creaminess and protein.
2. Add Nuts (Optional): If I want some crunch, I might add a small sprinkle of nuts or seeds, but I'll need to count the points for these additions.

Cauliflower Rice Breakfast Bowl with Sautéed Vegetables and Fresh Herbs

This Cauliflower Rice Breakfast Bowl with Sautéed Vegetables and Fresh Herbs is a nutritious, low-calorie way to start the day. By using cauliflower rice as a base, this dish is packed with fiber and vitamins while keeping the meal light and filling. The sautéed vegetables and fresh herbs add color, flavor, and a satisfying texture, making it an ideal breakfast choice that fits perfectly into the Zero Point Weight Loss program.

Prep time: 10 minutes | Cooking time: 20 minutes | Servings: 2

Ingredients (0 points):

- 2 cups cauliflower rice
- 1/2 cup red bell pepper, diced
- 1/2 cup zucchini, diced
- 1/4 cup onion, finely chopped
- 1 clove garlic, minced
- 1 tablespoon fresh parsley or cilantro, chopped
- Salt and pepper to taste
- Cooking spray or a small amount of water for sautéing

Step-by-Step Directions:

1. Prepare the Vegetables: I start by dicing the red bell pepper, zucchini, and onion. I also mince the garlic and chop the fresh herbs.
2. Cook the Cauliflower Rice: In a non-stick pan, I lightly spray cooking spray or add a small amount of water and heat it over medium heat. I add the cauliflower rice to the pan and cook it for about 5 minutes, stirring occasionally, until it's tender and slightly golden. Once cooked, I transfer the cauliflower rice to a bowl and set it aside.
3. Sauté the Vegetables: Using the same pan, I add the diced onion and garlic, cooking them for about 2 minutes until they're fragrant. I then add the diced red bell pepper and zucchini, sautéing them for another 3-5 minutes until the vegetables are tender but still crisp.
4. Combine and Season: I return the cooked cauliflower rice to the pan with the sautéed vegetables, stirring everything together until well combined. I season the mixture with salt and pepper to taste.
5. Serve: I divide the cauliflower rice and vegetable mixture between two bowls. I top each bowl with a sprinkle of fresh parsley or cilantro for added flavor and freshness.

Tips:

1. Extra Veggies: If I want to add more variety, I can include other zero-point vegetables like mushrooms, spinach, or cherry tomatoes.
2. Protein Boost: For added protein, I can top the bowl with a poached egg or a serving of lean chicken breast, but I'll need to count any additional points.
3. Make it Spicy: If I like a bit of heat, I can add a dash of hot sauce or red pepper flakes to the bowl.

Nutritional Information:

- Calories: 80, Protein: 3g, Fat: 0g, Carbohydrates: 14g, Fiber: 5g, Sugar: 6g, Points: 0

Serving Suggestions:

1. Top with Avocado (Optional): For a creamy texture, I might add a few slices of avocado, but I'll need to account for the points.
2. I often pair this bowl with a side of fresh fruit like orange slices or berries to round out the meal.

Baked Tomato and Egg Cups with Fresh Basil and Oregano

This Baked Tomato and Egg Cups recipe is a simple, flavorful breakfast that's both healthy and satisfying. By using tomatoes as a natural "cup" to hold the eggs, I can enjoy a protein-rich meal that's also full of fresh, herby goodness. The combination of fresh basil and oregano adds a burst of flavor, making this dish feel indulgent while still fitting perfectly within the Zero Point Weight Loss program.

Prep time: 10 minutes | Cooking time: 20 minutes | Servings: 2 (makes 4 tomato egg cups)

Ingredients (0 points):

- 4 medium tomatoes
- 4 large eggs
- 2 tablespoons fresh basil, chopped
- 1 teaspoon dried oregano (or 1 tablespoon fresh oregano, chopped)
- Salt and pepper to taste
- Cooking spray

Step-by-Step Directions:

1. Preheat the Oven: I preheat my oven to 375°F (190°C) and lightly spray a baking dish with cooking spray to prevent sticking.
2. Prepare the Tomatoes: I start by slicing the tops off the tomatoes and carefully scooping out the seeds and some of the flesh to create a hollow space for the eggs. I make sure not to pierce the skin so that the tomatoes hold their shape during baking.
3. Season the Tomatoes: Inside each hollowed tomato, I sprinkle a pinch of salt, pepper, and a little dried oregano. This step adds flavor to the tomatoes before I add the eggs.
4. Crack the Eggs into the Tomatoes: I crack one egg into each prepared tomato, being careful not to break the yolk. If the eggs are too large, I might remove a little of the egg white to prevent overflow.
5. Bake: I place the filled tomatoes in the prepared baking dish and bake them in the preheated oven for about 15-20 minutes, or until the egg whites are set but the yolks are still slightly runny (or to my preferred level of doneness).
6. Add Fresh Herbs: Once the tomatoes are done baking, I remove them from the oven and sprinkle the tops with the chopped fresh basil and a little more oregano if desired.
7. Serve: I serve the baked tomato and egg cups immediately while they're warm. They make a beautiful and nutritious breakfast that's both filling and fresh.

Tips:

1. Add Cheese (Optional): For a richer flavor, I can add a sprinkle of grated Parmesan or mozzarella cheese on top of the eggs before baking, but I'll need to count the points for the cheese.
2. Use Different Herbs: If I want to switch up the flavors, I can use other fresh herbs like thyme or chives in place of basil and oregano.
3. Prevent Spillage: If the tomatoes seem unstable in the baking dish, I can place them in a muffin tin to keep them upright during baking.

Nutritional Information:

- Calories: 130, Protein: 11g, Fat: 7g, Carbohydrates: 6g, Fiber: 2g, Sugar: 4g, Points: 0

Serving Suggestions:

1. Pair with a Side Salad: I like to serve these baked tomato and egg cups with a side of mixed greens or arugula tossed in a light vinaigrette for a complete meal.
2. Whole Grain Toast (Optional): For a heartier breakfast, I might add a slice of whole grain toast, but I'll be sure to count the points.

LUNCH RECIPES

Grilled Chicken Salad with Mixed Greens, Cucumber, Cherry Tomatoes, and Balsamic Vinegar

This Grilled Chicken Salad is a light yet satisfying lunch that's perfect for staying on track with my weight loss goals. It combines lean, grilled chicken breast with a variety of fresh vegetables, all served over a bed of mixed greens and drizzled with balsamic vinegar. This recipe is not only delicious but also fits perfectly within the Zero Point Weight Loss program, making it a go-to option for a healthy and balanced meal.

Prep time: 10 minutes | Cooking time: 10 minutes (grilling the chicken) | Servings: 2

Ingredients (0 points):

- 2 skinless, boneless chicken breasts
- 4 cups mixed greens (such as spinach, arugula, and romaine)
- 1 cup cucumber, sliced
- 1 cup cherry tomatoes, halved
- 2 tablespoons balsamic vinegar
- 1 clove garlic, minced
- Salt and pepper to taste
- Cooking spray

Step-by-Step Directions:

1. Prepare the Chicken: I start by preheating my grill or grill pan over medium-high heat. While it's heating, I season the chicken breasts with a pinch of salt, pepper, and minced garlic on both sides.
2. Grill the Chicken: I lightly spray the grill or grill pan with cooking spray to prevent sticking. I then place the seasoned chicken breasts on the grill and cook them for about 5-6 minutes on each side, or until the internal temperature reaches 165°F (75°C) and the chicken is cooked through.Once done, I remove the chicken from the grill and let it rest for a few minutes before slicing it into thin strips.
3. Prepare the Salad: While the chicken is grilling, I prepare the salad. I start by placing 2 cups of mixed greens on each plate. I then top the greens with the sliced cucumber and halved cherry tomatoes.
4. Assemble the Salad: I arrange the sliced grilled chicken on top of the vegetables. Finally, I drizzle 1 tablespoon of balsamic vinegar over each salad for a tangy finish.
5. Serve: The salad is ready to enjoy! It's a fresh, flavorful, and satisfying lunch that's perfect for any day of the week.

Tips:

1. Marinate the Chicken: For extra flavor, I can marinate the chicken breasts in a mixture of balsamic vinegar, garlic, and herbs for 30 minutes before grilling.
2. Add Extra Veggies: If I want to bulk up the salad, I can add other zero-point vegetables like bell peppers, radishes, or red onion slices.
3. Balsamic Reduction (Optional): To intensify the flavor of the balsamic vinegar, I can reduce it by simmering it in a small saucepan until it thickens slightly.

Nutritional Information:

- Calories: 180, Protein: 30g, Fat: 2g, Carbohydrates: 8g, Fiber: 3g, Sugar: 5g, Points: 0

Serving Suggestions:

1. Pair with a Light Soup: This salad pairs well with a light vegetable soup for a more filling meal, especially on cooler days.
2. Add a Side of Fruit: I sometimes enjoy this salad with a side of fresh fruit like apple slices or a handful of berries for a sweet complement to the savory flavors.

Spaghetti Squash with Marinara Sauce and Sautéed Vegetables (Zucchini, Mushrooms, and Spinach)

This Spaghetti Squash with Marinara Sauce and Sautéed Vegetables is a delicious and satisfying lunch that's perfect for staying on track with my weight loss goals. Spaghetti squash serves as a low-calorie alternative to pasta, while the marinara sauce and sautéed vegetables add rich flavor and nutrients.

Prep time: 15 minutes | Cooking time: 45 minutes (includes roasting the spaghetti squash) | Servings: 2

Ingredients (0 points):

- 1 medium spaghetti squash
- 1 cup marinara sauce (ensure it's a low-sugar, no-oil-added variety)
- 1 cup zucchini, diced
- 1 cup mushrooms, sliced
- 2 cups fresh spinach
- 2 cloves garlic, minced
- Cooking spray or a small amount of water for sautéing
- Salt and pepper to taste
- Optional: fresh basil or parsley, chopped

Step-by-Step Directions:

1. Prepare the Spaghetti Squash: I start by preheating my oven to 400°F (200°C). I then cut the spaghetti squash in half lengthwise and scoop out the seeds. I lightly spray the cut sides with cooking spray and season with a pinch of salt and pepper. I place the squash halves cut-side down on a baking sheet and roast them in the oven for about 40-45 minutes, or until the flesh is tender and easily pulled apart with a fork. Once cooked, I set the squash aside to cool slightly before scraping out the strands with a fork to create "spaghetti."
2. Prepare the Sautéed Vegetables: While the squash is roasting, I prepare the vegetables. In a large non-stick pan, I lightly spray cooking spray or add a small amount of water and heat it over medium heat. I sauté the minced garlic for about 30 seconds until fragrant. I then add the diced zucchini and sliced mushrooms to the pan and cook them for about 5 minutes until they're tender. Finally, I add the fresh spinach and cook for another 1-2 minutes until the spinach is wilted.
3. Heat the Marinara Sauce: I pour the marinara sauce into a small saucepan and heat it over low to medium heat until it's warmed through. I can season the sauce with additional herbs or spices if I like.
4. Combine and Serve: I divide the cooked spaghetti squash between two plates, topping each portion with the sautéed vegetables. I then ladle the warm marinara sauce over the top and garnish with fresh basil or parsley if desired.
5. Enjoy: The dish is ready to enjoy! It's a filling, flavorful, and healthy lunch that's perfect for keeping me satisfied and on track with my weight loss goals.

Tips:

1. If I like a bit of heat, I can add a pinch of red pepper flakes to the marinara sauce while it's heating.
2. Roasting the Squash: To save time, I can roast the spaghetti squash ahead of time and store the strands in the refrigerator until I'm ready to use them.
3. Add Protein: For added protein, I can top the dish with grilled chicken or shrimp, but I'll need to count the points for the protein.

Nutritional Information:

- Calories: 160, Protein: 6g, Fat: 1g, Carbohydrates: 35g, Fiber: 7g, Sugar: 12g, Points: 0

Serving Suggestions:

1. Pair with a Side Salad: I like to serve this dish with a simple side salad of mixed greens and a light vinaigrette for a more complete meal.

Tuna Salad Lettuce Wraps with Diced Celery, Red Onion, and Fresh Herbs

These Tuna Salad Lettuce Wraps are a light, refreshing, and satisfying lunch option that's perfect for sticking to my weight loss goals. By using lettuce leaves as a wrap, I keep the meal low in calories and carbs while still enjoying a hearty and flavorful tuna salad. This recipe is quick to prepare, full of fresh flavors, and fits perfectly into the Zero Point Weight Loss program.

Prep time: 10 minutes | Cooking time: None | Servings: 2 (makes 4 lettuce wraps)

Ingredients (0 points):

- 1 can (5 oz) tuna in water, drained
- 1/2 cup celery, diced
- 1/4 cup red onion, finely chopped
- 2 tablespoons fresh parsley, chopped
- 1 tablespoon fresh dill, chopped
- 1 tablespoon lemon juice
- Salt and pepper to taste
- 4 large lettuce leaves (such as romaine or butter lettuce)

Step-by-Step Directions:

2. Prepare the Tuna Salad: I start by draining the tuna and placing it in a medium mixing bowl. I use a fork to break it up into smaller Pieces. Next, I add the diced celery, finely chopped red onion, fresh parsley, and dill to the bowl. I squeeze in the lemon juice and season the mixture with a pinch of salt and pepper.
3. Mix the Ingredients (0 points): I thoroughly mix all the ingredients together until the tuna salad is well combined and the flavors are evenly distributed. If I like my tuna salad creamier, I could add a tablespoon of fat-free Greek yogurt or mustard, but I'll ensure it stays within the zero-point guidelines.
4. Assemble the Lettuce Wraps: I lay out the large lettuce leaves on a plate. I then divide the tuna salad mixture evenly among the four lettuce leaves, placing the salad in the center of each leaf.I gently fold the sides of the lettuce leaves over the tuna salad to create a wrap.
5. Serve: The lettuce wraps are ready to eat! They're a fresh, healthy, and satisfying lunch that's perfect for enjoying at home or on the go.

Tips:

1. Add Crunch: For extra crunch, I can add a few slices of radish or cucumber to the wraps.
2. Spice it Up: If I like a bit of heat, I can add a pinch of red pepper flakes or a dash of hot sauce to the tuna salad.
3. Keep it Fresh: To prevent the lettuce from wilting, I prepare the tuna salad ahead of time and assemble the wraps just before serving.

Nutritional Information:

- Calories: 120, Protein: 20g, Fat: 1g, Carbohydrates: 6g, Fiber: 2g, Sugar: 2g, Points: 0

Serving Suggestions:

1. Pair with a Side of Fresh Fruit: I like to enjoy these wraps with a side of fresh fruit like apple slices or a handful of berries for a complete meal.
2. Serve with a Light Soup: These wraps also pair well with a light vegetable soup, especially on cooler days.

Grilled Shrimp Skewers with a Side of Roasted Asparagus and Bell Peppers

This Grilled Shrimp Skewers with Roasted Asparagus and Bell Peppers recipe is a light, flavorful, and satisfying lunch that's perfect for staying on track with my weight loss goals. The shrimp is marinated with simple seasonings, grilled to perfection, and paired with a side of roasted asparagus and bell peppers. This meal is packed with protein and vibrant vegetables, making it a delicious option within the Zero Point Weight Loss program.

Prep time: 15 minutes | Cooking time: 15 minutes (grilling the shrimp and roasting the vegetables) | Servings: 2

Ingredients (0 points):

- 12 large shrimp, peeled and deveined
- 1 cup asparagus, trimmed
- 1 cup bell peppers, sliced (any color)
- 2 cloves garlic, minced
- 1 tablespoon fresh lemon juice
- 1 tablespoon fresh parsley, chopped
- 1 teaspoon paprika
- Salt and pepper to taste
- Cooking spray or a small amount of water for grilling and roasting

Step-by-Step Directions:

1. Marinate the Shrimp: I start by preparing the shrimp. In a bowl, I toss the shrimp with minced garlic, lemon juice, paprika, and a pinch of salt and pepper. I let the shrimp marinate for about 10 minutes while I prepare the vegetables.
2. Prepare the Vegetables: I preheat my oven to 400°F (200°C). I then trim the asparagus and slice the bell peppers. I place the vegetables on a baking sheet, lightly spray them with cooking spray, and season with salt and pepper.
3. Roast the Vegetables: I roast the asparagus and bell peppers in the preheated oven for about 12-15 minutes, or until they are tender and slightly caramelized. I make sure to toss the vegetables halfway through cooking to ensure even roasting.
4. Grill the Shrimp: While the vegetables are roasting, I preheat my grill or grill pan over medium-high heat. I thread the marinated shrimp onto skewers and lightly spray them with cooking spray to prevent sticking. I grill the shrimp skewers for about 2-3 minutes on each side, or until the shrimp are opaque and cooked through. Once done, I remove the shrimp from the grill and set them aside.
5. Serve: I divide the roasted asparagus and bell peppers between two plates. I then place the grilled shrimp skewers on top and sprinkle the dish with fresh parsley for a burst of color and flavor. The dish is ready to enjoy immediately.

Tips:

1. If I don't have a grill, I can cook the shrimp in a non-stick skillet over medium-high heat.
2. Add Spice: For a spicier kick, I can add a pinch of red pepper flakes to the shrimp marinade.
3. If using wooden skewers, I soak them in water for about 20 minutes before grilling to prevent burning.

Nutritional Information:

- Calories: 150, Protein: 22g, Fat: 2g, Carbohydrates: 10g, Fiber: 3g, Sugar: 4g, Points: 0

Serving Suggestions:

1. Pair with a Side Salad: I like to serve this dish with a side of mixed greens or a cucumber and tomato salad for added freshness.
2. Add a Light Dressing: A squeeze of fresh lemon juice or a drizzle of balsamic vinegar over the roasted vegetables adds extra flavor without adding points.

Turkey and Cabbage Stir-Fry with Ginger and Garlic

This Turkey and Cabbage Stir-Fry with Ginger and Garlic is a flavorful, low-calorie lunch that's both satisfying and nutritious. The lean turkey provides a high-protein base, while the cabbage adds crunch and volume. Fresh ginger and garlic bring warmth and depth to the dish, making it a delicious option that fits perfectly into the Zero Point Weight Loss program.

Prep time: 10 minutes | Cooking time: 15 minutes | Servings: 2

Ingredients (0 points):

- 8 oz lean ground turkey (99% fat-free)
- 3 cups green cabbage, thinly sliced
- 1/2 cup onion, finely chopped
- 1/2 cup bell pepper, sliced
- 2 cloves garlic, minced
- 1 tablespoon fresh ginger, minced
- 2 tablespoons soy sauce (low-sodium)
- 1 tablespoon rice vinegar
- 1/4 teaspoon red pepper flakes (optional)
- Cooking spray or a small amount of water for sautéing
- Fresh cilantro or green onions for garnish (optional)

Step-by-Step Directions:

1. Prepare the Ingredients (0 points): I begin by preparing all the vegetables. I thinly slice the cabbage, finely chop the onion, slice the bell pepper, and mince the garlic and ginger.
2. Cook the Ground Turkey: In a large non-stick skillet or wok, I lightly spray cooking spray or add a small amount of water and heat it over medium-high heat. I add the ground turkey to the skillet, breaking it up with a spatula as it cooks. I cook the turkey for about 5-7 minutes, until it's no longer pink and fully cooked. I then remove the turkey from the skillet and set it aside.
3. Sauté the Vegetables: In the same skillet, I add a bit more cooking spray or water if needed and then add the minced garlic and ginger. I sauté them for about 30 seconds until fragrant. Next, I add the chopped onion and sliced bell pepper to the skillet and cook for about 3 minutes until they begin to soften. I then add the sliced cabbage to the skillet, stirring everything together. I continue to cook the vegetables for another 5-7 minutes until the cabbage is tender but still slightly crisp.
4. Combine and Season: I return the cooked turkey to the skillet with the vegetables. I then pour in the soy sauce and rice vinegar, stirring everything together until well combined. If I'm using red pepper flakes, I add them at this stage for a bit of heat. I cook the stir-fry for an additional 2 minutes to ensure all the flavors meld together.
5. Serve: I divide the turkey and cabbage stir-fry between two plates. If I'm using fresh cilantro or green onions, I sprinkle them on top for garnish. The dish is ready to enjoy immediately.

Tips:

1. I can bulk up the dish with other zero-point vegetables like mushrooms, snap peas, or broccoli.
2. Adjust the Spice: If I prefer a milder dish, I can omit the red pepper flakes. For more heat, I can increase the amount or add a drizzle of hot sauce.
3. This stir-fry reheats well, so I can prepare it ahead of time and enjoy it for lunch the next day.

Nutritional Information:

- Calories: 160, Protein: 28g, Fat: 3g, Carbohydrates: 10g, Fiber: 4g, Sugar: 4g, Points: 0

Serving Suggestions:

1. I like to pair this stir-fry with cauliflower rice for a more filling meal while still keeping it zero points.
2. Add a Side Salad: A simple side salad with a light vinaigrette complements the flavors of the stir-fry and adds more fresh vegetables to the meal.

Roasted Vegetable Soup with Butternut Squash, Carrots, and Leeks

This Roasted Vegetable Soup with Butternut Squash, Carrots, and Leeks is a warm and comforting lunch option that's perfect for keeping me full and satisfied without adding any points. Roasting the vegetables before blending them into the soup brings out their natural sweetness and adds depth to the flavor. This hearty soup is easy to make, packed with nutrients, and fits perfectly into the Zero Point Weight Loss program.

Prep time: 15 minutes | Cooking time: 45 minutes | Servings: 2

Ingredients (0 points):

- 2 cups butternut squash, peeled and cubed
- 2 large carrots, peeled and sliced
- 1 large leek, white and light green parts only, sliced
- 2 cloves garlic, minced
- 1 teaspoon fresh thyme, chopped (or 1/2 teaspoon dried thyme)
- 1 teaspoon fresh rosemary, chopped (or 1/2 teaspoon dried rosemary)
- 4 cups vegetable broth
- Cooking spray
- Salt and pepper to taste
- Optional: fresh parsley for garnish

Step-by-Step Directions:

1. Preheat the Oven: I start by preheating my oven to 400°F (200°C).
2. Prepare the Vegetables: I peel and cube the butternut squash, peel and slice the carrots, and slice the leeks. I make sure to wash the leeks thoroughly to remove any grit. I then place the prepared vegetables on a large baking sheet.
3. Season and Roast the Vegetables: I lightly spray the vegetables with cooking spray and sprinkle them with chopped thyme, rosemary, salt, and pepper. I toss everything together to ensure the vegetables are evenly coated with the herbs and seasoning. I roast the vegetables in the preheated oven for about 25-30 minutes, or until they are tender and slightly caramelized, stirring halfway through to ensure even roasting.
4. Blend the Soup: Once the vegetables are roasted, I transfer them to a large pot. I add the minced garlic and pour in the vegetable broth. Using an immersion blender, I blend the soup until it reaches a smooth and creamy consistency. If I don't have an immersion blender, I can carefully blend the soup in batches in a regular blender, then return it to the pot.
5. Simmer and Adjust Seasoning: I bring the soup to a gentle simmer over medium heat and let it cook for another 10 minutes to allow the flavors to meld together. I taste the soup and adjust the seasoning with additional salt and pepper if needed.
6. Serve: I ladle the soup into bowls, garnish with fresh parsley if desired, and enjoy it warm. It's a comforting, nutritious lunch that's perfect for any day of the week.

Tips:

1. Customize the Vegetables: I can add or substitute other zero-point vegetables like sweet potatoes, parsnips, or celery for a different flavor profile.
2. For a bit of heat, I can add a pinch of red pepper flakes or a dash of hot sauce while blending the soup.
3. Storage: This soup keeps well in the refrigerator for up to 3 days and can also be frozen for up to a month, making it great for meal prep.

Nutritional Information:

- Calories: 120, Protein: 4g, Fat: 1g, Carbohydrates: 26g, Fiber: 7g, Sugar: 8g, Points: 0

Serving Suggestions:

1. Pair with a Salad: I like to enjoy this soup with a simple green salad or a side of roasted vegetables for a more complete meal.

Baked Cod with a Side of Steamed Broccoli and Lemon-Garlic Sauce

This Baked Cod with a Side of Steamed Broccoli and Lemon-Garlic Sauce is a light, flavorful, and protein-rich lunch option that's perfect for keeping me on track with my weight loss goals. The cod is baked to perfection with simple seasonings, while the steamed broccoli adds a nutritious and satisfying side. The zesty lemon-garlic sauce ties everything together, making this meal both delicious and fitting perfectly into the Zero Point Weight Loss program.

Prep time: 10 minutes | Cooking time: 20 minutes | Servings: 2

Ingredients (0 points):

- 2 cod fillets (about 4 oz each)
- 2 cups broccoli florets
- 2 cloves garlic, minced
- 1 tablespoon fresh lemon juice
- 1 teaspoon lemon zest
- 1 tablespoon fresh parsley, chopped
- Cooking spray
- Salt and pepper to taste

Step-by-Step Directions:

2. Preheat the Oven: I start by preheating my oven to 375°F (190°C). While the oven is heating, I prepare the cod fillets.
3. Prepare the Cod: I lightly spray a baking dish with cooking spray to prevent sticking. I place the cod fillets in the dish and season them with a pinch of salt and pepper. I sprinkle half of the minced garlic over the fillets.
4. Bake the Cod: I bake the cod fillets in the preheated oven for about 15-20 minutes, or until the fish is opaque and flakes easily with a fork. The exact time may vary depending on the thickness of the fillets.
5. Steam the Broccoli: While the cod is baking, I steam the broccoli florets. I place the broccoli in a steamer basket over boiling water and cover it with a lid. I steam the broccoli for about 5-7 minutes, or until it's tender but still bright green.
6. Prepare the Lemon-Garlic Sauce: In a small bowl, I combine the remaining minced garlic, fresh lemon juice, lemon zest, and chopped parsley. I stir everything together to create a simple, flavorful sauce.
7. Serve: Once the cod is cooked, I remove it from the oven and drizzle the lemon-garlic sauce over the top. I divide the steamed broccoli between two plates and serve it alongside the baked cod. The dish is ready to enjoy immediately.

Tips:

1. Add Extra Flavor: If I want to add a bit more flavor to the cod, I can sprinkle some paprika or dried herbs like thyme or oregano before baking.
2. Make it Spicy: For a touch of heat, I can add a pinch of red pepper flakes to the lemon-garlic sauce.
3. Cook the Broccoli to Taste: If I prefer my broccoli more tender, I can steam it for an additional minute or two.

Nutritional Information:

- Calories: 140, Protein: 28g, Fat: 2g, Carbohydrates: 8g, Fiber: 4g, Sugar: 2g, Points: 0

Serving Suggestions:

1. Pair with a Side Salad: I like to pair this dish with a light side salad of mixed greens and a lemon vinaigrette to complement the flavors of the cod.
2. Serve with Cauliflower Rice: For a more filling meal, I sometimes serve this dish with cauliflower rice, keeping the entire meal at zero points.

Chickpea and Veggie Salad with Cucumber, Cherry Tomatoes, Red Onion, and Fresh Parsley

This Chickpea and Veggie Salad is a fresh, vibrant, and satisfying lunch that's perfect for keeping me on track with my weight loss goals. The combination of chickpeas, crunchy vegetables, and fresh herbs creates a dish that's not only nutritious but also full of flavor. This salad is quick to prepare, light yet filling, and fits seamlessly into the Zero Point Weight Loss program.

Prep time: 15 minutes | Cooking time: None | Servings: 2

Ingredients (0 points):

- 1 can (15 oz) chickpeas, drained and rinsed
- 1 cup cucumber, diced
- 1 cup cherry tomatoes, halved
- 1/4 cup red onion, finely chopped
- 1/4 cup fresh parsley, chopped
- 1 tablespoon fresh lemon juice
- 1 teaspoon olive oil (optional, but 1 point if used)
- Salt and pepper to taste

Step-by-Step Directions:

1. Prepare the Ingredients: I start by draining and rinsing the chickpeas. I then dice the cucumber, halve the cherry tomatoes, finely chop the red onion, and chop the fresh parsley.
2. Assemble the Salad: In a large mixing bowl, I combine the chickpeas, diced cucumber, cherry tomatoes, red onion, and fresh parsley. I toss everything together to mix the ingredients evenly.
3. Add the Dressing: I drizzle the fresh lemon juice over the salad, which adds a bright, tangy flavor. If I choose to use olive oil, I drizzle it over the salad as well. I then season the salad with a pinch of salt and pepper to taste.
4. Toss and Serve: I gently toss the salad to ensure that the dressing and seasonings are evenly distributed. I then divide the salad into two portions and serve it immediately. It's a refreshing and nutritious lunch that's perfect for any day.

Tips:

1. Add Extra Veggies: If I want to bulk up the salad, I can add other zero-point vegetables like bell peppers, shredded carrots, or sliced radishes.
2. Make it a Meal: For added protein, I can top the salad with grilled chicken or shrimp, but I'll need to count the points for these additions.
3. Chill Before Serving: If I have time, I like to chill the salad in the refrigerator for about 15 minutes before serving. This helps the flavors meld together and makes the salad even more refreshing.

Nutritional Information:

- Calories: 180, Protein: 8g, Fat: 2g, Carbohydrates: 32g, Fiber: 9g, Sugar: 5g, Points: 0 (if olive oil is omitted)

Serving Suggestions:

1. Pair with a Light Soup: This salad pairs well with a light vegetable soup for a more filling meal, especially on cooler days.
2. Serve with Whole Grain Crackers: For added texture, I sometimes enjoy this salad with a few whole grain crackers on the side (points counted separately).

Grilled Turkey Patties with Sautéed Spinach and Mushrooms

This Grilled Turkey Patties with Sautéed Spinach and Mushrooms recipe is a protein-packed, flavorful lunch option that's perfect for keeping me on track with my weight loss goals. The lean turkey patties are seasoned simply and grilled to perfection, while the sautéed spinach and mushrooms provide a nutrient-rich, satisfying side. This meal is light, filling, and fits seamlessly into the Zero Point Weight Loss program.

Prep time: 10 minutes | Cooking time: 15 minutes | Servings: 2

Ingredients (0 points):

- 8 oz lean ground turkey (99% fat-free)
- 1 cup mushrooms, sliced
- 4 cups fresh spinach
- 1 clove garlic, minced
- 1 tablespoon fresh parsley, chopped
- 1 teaspoon onion powder
- 1 teaspoon garlic powder
- Salt and pepper to taste
- Cooking spray or a small amount of water for sautéing and grilling

Step-by-Step Directions:

1. Prepare the Turkey Patties: I start by mixing the lean ground turkey in a bowl with onion powder, garlic powder, a pinch of salt, and pepper. I ensure the seasoning is evenly distributed throughout the meat. I then form the mixture into two equal-sized patties, making sure they are not too thick to allow even cooking.
2. Grill the Turkey Patties: I preheat my grill or grill pan over medium-high heat. Once hot, I lightly spray the grill with cooking spray to prevent sticking. I place the turkey patties on the grill and cook them for about 5-6 minutes on each side, or until the internal temperature reaches 165°F (75°C) and the patties are fully cooked. Once done, I set the patties aside to rest.
3. Sauté the Vegetables: While the turkey patties are grilling, I prepare the sautéed spinach and mushrooms. In a large non-stick skillet, I lightly spray cooking spray or add a small amount of water and heat it over medium heat. I add the minced garlic to the skillet and sauté it for about 30 seconds until fragrant. Next, I add the sliced mushrooms to the skillet and cook them for about 5 minutes, or until they release their moisture and start to brown. I then add the fresh spinach to the skillet and sauté for another 2-3 minutes until it's wilted. I season the vegetables with a pinch of salt and pepper to taste.
4. Serve: I divide the sautéed spinach and mushrooms between two plates, placing one turkey patty on each plate. I sprinkle the chopped parsley over the top as a garnish. The dish is ready to enjoy immediately.

Tips:

1. Add Spice: If I like a bit of heat, I can add a pinch of red pepper flakes to the turkey mixture or the sautéed vegetables.
2. Make it a Meal: For added variety, I can serve this dish with a side of roasted vegetables or a small salad.
3. Customize the Patties: I can mix in fresh herbs like thyme or rosemary into the turkey mixture for additional flavor.

Nutritional Information:

- Calories: 180, Protein: 30g, Fat: 3g, Carbohydrates: 8g, Fiber: 4g, Sugar: 3g, Points: 0

Serving Suggestions:

1. Pair with a Side Salad: I like to serve this dish with a simple side salad made of mixed greens and a light vinaigrette to keep the meal fresh and light.
2. Serve with Cauliflower Rice: For a more substantial meal, I sometimes add a side of cauliflower rice, which also keeps the meal at zero points.

Zucchini Noodles with Tomato Basil Sauce and Grilled Chicken Strips

This recipe is a light, flavorful, and satisfying lunch that's perfect for keeping me on track with my weight loss goals. Zucchini noodles (also known as zoodles) are a fantastic low-carb alternative to traditional pasta, and when paired with a fresh tomato basil sauce and lean grilled chicken, this meal becomes both nutritious and delicious.

Prep time: 10 minutes | Cooking time: 20 minutes | Servings: 2

Ingredients (0 points):

- 2 medium zucchini, spiralized into noodles
- 8 oz chicken breast, boneless and skinless
- 2 cups cherry tomatoes, halved
- 1/4 cup onion, finely chopped
- 2 cloves garlic, minced
- 1/4 cup fresh basil, chopped
- 1 tablespoon fresh lemon juice
- 1/2 teaspoon dried oregano
- Salt and pepper to taste
- Cooking spray or a small amount of water for grilling and sautéing

Step-by-Step Directions:

1. Prepare the Chicken: I start by seasoning the chicken breast with a pinch of salt, pepper, and dried oregano. I then preheat my grill or grill pan over medium-high heat. I lightly spray the grill with cooking spray to prevent sticking. I place the chicken breast on the grill and cook for about 5-6 minutes on each side, or until the chicken is fully cooked and reaches an internal temperature of 165°F (75°C). Once the chicken is done, I remove it from the grill and let it rest for a few minutes before slicing it into thin strips.
2. Make the Tomato Basil Sauce: While the chicken is grilling, I prepare the tomato basil sauce. In a large non-stick skillet, I lightly spray cooking spray or add a small amount of water and heat it over medium heat. I add the minced garlic and chopped onion to the skillet, sautéing them for about 2-3 minutes until they become fragrant and the onion is softened. I then add the halved cherry tomatoes to the skillet and cook them for about 5-7 minutes, or until they start to break down and release their juices. I season the sauce with a pinch of salt and pepper to taste. Finally, I stir in the fresh basil and lemon juice, allowing the flavors to meld together for another 1-2 minutes.
3. Prepare the Zucchini Noodles: I spiralize the zucchini into noodles (zoodles) using a spiralizer. If I don't have a spiralizer, I can use a vegetable peeler to create long, thin strips. I add the zucchini noodles to the skillet with the tomato basil sauce, tossing them gently to coat the noodles evenly with the sauce. I cook the zoodles for about 2-3 minutes, just until they are tender but still slightly crisp.
4. Assemble the Dish: I divide the zucchini noodles with tomato basil sauce between two plates. I then top each plate with the sliced grilled chicken strips.
5. Serve: The dish is ready to enjoy immediately. It's a fresh, flavorful, and satisfying lunch that's perfect for any day of the week.

Tips:

1. Add Extra Veggies: I can bulk up the dish by adding other zero-point vegetables like spinach, bell peppers, or mushrooms to the tomato basil sauce.
2. Make it Spicy: For a bit of heat, I can add a pinch of red pepper flakes to the sauce while it's cooking.
3. I cook the zucchini noodles just until they are tender to avoid them becoming too watery.

Nutritional Information:

- Calories: 180, Protein: 30g, Fat: 2g, Carbohydrates: 10g, Fiber: 4g, Sugar: 6g, Points: 0

Serving Suggestions:

1. Pair with a Side Salad: I like to serve this dish with a simple green salad dressed with lemon vinaigrette for a light and refreshing meal.

Spicy Black Bean Soup with Diced Tomatoes, Onions, and Cilantro

This Spicy Black Bean Soup is a hearty, flavorful lunch option that's perfect for staying on track with my weight loss goals. The black beans provide a rich source of protein and fiber, while the diced tomatoes, onions, and cilantro add freshness and depth to the dish. With a touch of spice, this soup is both satisfying and invigorating, making it an ideal choice for a warming meal that fits perfectly into the Zero Point Weight Loss program.

Prep time: 10 minutes | Cooking time: 25 minutes | Servings: 2

Ingredients (0 points):

- 1 can (15 oz) black beans, drained and rinsed
- 1 cup diced tomatoes (canned or fresh)
- 1/2 cup onion, finely chopped
- 2 cloves garlic, minced
- 1 jalapeño pepper, seeded and minced (optional, for spice)
- 1 teaspoon ground cumin
- 1/2 teaspoon smoked paprika
- 4 cups vegetable broth
- 1/4 cup fresh cilantro, chopped
- 1 tablespoon fresh lime juice
- Salt and pepper to taste
- Cooking spray or a small amount of water for sautéing

Step-by-Step Directions:

1. Prepare the Vegetables: I start by finely chopping the onion, mincing the garlic, and seeding and mincing the jalapeño pepper if I'm using it. I also chop the cilantro and set it aside for later.
2. Sauté the Aromatics: In a large pot or Dutch oven, I lightly spray cooking spray or add a small amount of water and heat it over medium heat. I add the chopped onion, garlic, and jalapeño to the pot and sauté them for about 3-5 minutes until the onion is soft and translucent.
3. Add the Tomatoes and Spices: I then add the diced tomatoes, ground cumin, and smoked paprika to the pot. I stir everything together, allowing the spices to coat the vegetables and cook for another 2 minutes to deepen the flavors.
4. Add the Black Beans and Broth: I pour the drained and rinsed black beans into the pot, followed by the vegetable broth. I stir the soup to combine all the ingredients and bring it to a simmer over medium heat. I let the soup cook for about 15 minutes, allowing the flavors to meld together.
5. Blend the Soup (Optional): If I prefer a creamier texture, I can use an immersion blender to partially blend the soup, leaving some beans whole for texture. If I like my soup chunkier, I can skip this step.
6. Finish with Fresh Lime and Cilantro: Once the soup is cooked, I stir in the fresh lime juice and chopped cilantro. I taste the soup and adjust the seasoning with additional salt and pepper if needed.
7. Serve: I divide the soup between two bowls, garnishing each with a sprinkle of fresh cilantro. The soup is ready to enjoy immediately, providing a warm and satisfying meal.

Tips:

1. If I want more heat, I can leave the seeds in the jalapeño or add a pinch of cayenne pepper. For a milder version, I can omit the jalapeño altogether. I can add other zero-point vegetables like bell peppers, carrots, or zucchini to the soup for added nutrition and volume.
2. This soup stores well in the refrigerator for up to 3 days, making it a great option for meal prep.

Nutritional Information:

- Calories: 180, Protein: 10g, Fat: 1g, Carbohydrates: 36g, Fiber: 13g, Sugar: 5g, Points: 0

Serving Suggestions:

1. I like to serve this soup with a simple green salad or a side of steamed vegetables for a more complete meal.
2. Top with Avocado (Optional): For a bit of creaminess, I sometimes add a few slices of avocado on top, but I'll need to count the points for the avocado.

Grilled Eggplant and Red Pepper Stack with Fresh Herbs and a Drizzle of Balsamic Vinegar

This Grilled Eggplant and Red Pepper Stack is a flavorful, visually appealing lunch that's both light and satisfying. By stacking layers of grilled eggplant and red pepper, and finishing with fresh herbs and a drizzle of balsamic vinegar, I can enjoy a meal that's full of Mediterranean flavors while staying within the Zero Point Weight Loss program. It's simple to make, delicious, and perfect for those days when I want something nutritious and elegant.

Prep time: 10 minutes | Cooking time: 15 minutes | Servings: 2

Ingredients (0 points):

- 1 medium eggplant, sliced into 1/2-inch rounds
- 1 large red bell pepper, cut into large flat pieces
- 2 cloves garlic, minced
- 1 tablespoon fresh basil, chopped
- 1 tablespoon fresh parsley, chopped
- 1 tablespoon balsamic vinegar
- Salt and pepper to taste
- Cooking spray or a small amount of water for grilling

Step-by-Step Directions:

1. Prepare the Vegetables: I start by slicing the eggplant into 1/2-inch thick rounds and cutting the red bell pepper into large, flat pieces. I lightly sprinkle both with salt and let them sit for about 5 minutes to draw out any excess moisture, then pat them dry with a paper towel.
2. Grill the Vegetables:cI preheat my grill or grill pan over medium-high heat. Once hot, I lightly spray the grill with cooking spray to prevent sticking. I place the eggplant rounds and red pepper pieces on the grill. I cook the eggplant for about 4-5 minutes on each side until it's tender and has nice grill marks. The red pepper should be grilled until the skin is charred and the flesh is softened, about 6-8 minutes total. Once grilled, I remove the vegetables from the heat and let them cool slightly.
3. Assemble the Stack: On each plate, I begin layering the grilled vegetables, starting with an eggplant round at the base. I top it with a piece of grilled red pepper, then continue to alternate layers of eggplant and red pepper until I've used all the vegetables. I sprinkle the minced garlic over the top of the stacks, followed by the chopped basil and parsley.
4. Drizzle with Balsamic Vinegar: To finish, I drizzle 1/2 tablespoon of balsamic vinegar over each vegetable stack. The vinegar adds a tangy sweetness that complements the smoky grilled vegetables.
5. Serve: The Grilled Eggplant and Red Pepper Stack is ready to enjoy immediately. It's a beautiful, nutritious lunch that's perfect for a light meal.

Tips:

1. I can experiment with other fresh herbs like thyme or oregano to change up the flavors.
2. Add Protein: For a more substantial meal, I can add grilled chicken or a poached egg to the stack, though I'll need to count the points for these additions.
3. Balsamic Glaze (Optional): For a more intense flavor, I can reduce the balsamic vinegar in a small saucepan until it thickens into a glaze before drizzling it over the stack.

Nutritional Information:

- Calories: 90, Protein: 2g, Fat: 0g, Carbohydrates: 20g, Fiber: 6g, Sugar: 10g, Points: 0

Serving Suggestions:

1. Pair with a Side Salad: I like to serve this stack with a light salad of mixed greens dressed with lemon juice or a light vinaigrette for a refreshing complement.

DINNER RECIPES

Baked Lemon Herb Chicken with Roasted Brussels Sprouts and Carrots

This is a delicious, comforting dinner option that's perfect for helping me stay on track with my weight loss goals. The chicken is marinated with fresh herbs and lemon, then baked to juicy perfection. It's paired with a side of roasted Brussels sprouts and carrots, which add a satisfying crunch and natural sweetness to the meal.

Prep time: 15 minutes | Cooking time: 30 minutes | Servings: 2

Ingredients (0 points):

- 2 boneless, skinless chicken breasts (about 4 oz each) (0 points)
- 2 cups Brussels sprouts, halved
- 2 large carrots, peeled and sliced into sticks
- 2 cloves garlic, minced
- 2 tablespoons fresh lemon juice
- 1 tablespoon fresh parsley, chopped
- 1 teaspoon dried oregano
- 1 teaspoon dried thyme
- Salt and pepper to taste
- Cooking spray or a small amount of water for roasting

Step-by-Step Directions:

1. Marinate the Chicken: I start by placing the chicken breasts in a resealable plastic bag or a shallow dish. I add the fresh lemon juice, minced garlic, dried oregano, dried thyme, and a pinch of salt and pepper. I seal the bag or cover the dish and let the chicken marinate in the refrigerator for at least 15 minutes, or up to a few hours if I have more time.
2. Preheat the Oven: While the chicken is marinating, I preheat my oven to 400°F (200°C).
3. Prepare the Vegetables: I halve the Brussels sprouts and peel and slice the carrots into sticks. I place the vegetables on a large baking sheet, lightly spray them with cooking spray, and season with salt and pepper. I toss the vegetables to coat them evenly.
4. Bake the Chicken and Roast the Vegetables: I place the marinated chicken breasts in a baking dish and put them in the preheated oven. I also place the baking sheet with the Brussels sprouts and carrots in the oven. I bake the chicken for about 25-30 minutes, or until the chicken is cooked through and reaches an internal temperature of 165°F (75°C). I roast the vegetables for the same amount of time, tossing them halfway through to ensure they cook evenly and develop a nice golden color.
5. Serve: Once the chicken and vegetables are done, I remove them from the oven. I let the chicken rest for a few minutes before slicing it. I then divide the chicken and vegetables between two plates. To finish, I sprinkle the chopped fresh parsley over the chicken and vegetables for added freshness and flavor.

Tips:

1. Add Extra Flavor: For more lemon flavor, I can add some lemon zest to the marinade or squeeze fresh lemon juice over the chicken just before serving.
2. Change Up the Herbs: I can use other fresh or dried herbs like rosemary or basil if I want to change up the flavors. If I like a bit of heat, I can add a pinch of red pepper flakes to the marinade.

Nutritional Information:

- Calories: 220, Protein: 28g, Fat: 2g, Carbohydrates: 20g, Fiber: 8g, Sugar: 7g, Points: 0

Serving Suggestions:

1. Pair with a Side Salad: I like to serve this dish with a simple green salad dressed with a light vinaigrette to keep the meal fresh and balanced.
2. Add a Grain (Optional): If I want a more filling meal, I can serve this dish with a side of quinoa or brown rice, but I'll need to count the points for the grains.

Shrimp and Vegetable Stir-Fry with Bell Peppers, Snow Peas, and Ginger

This is a quick, flavorful dinner that's perfect for keeping me on track with my weight loss goals. The dish combines succulent shrimp with vibrant bell peppers, crunchy snow peas, and fresh ginger, all stir-fried to perfection. It's light yet satisfying and fits seamlessly into the Zero Point Weight Loss program. This meal is not only easy to make but also packed with nutrients and flavor, making it an ideal choice for a healthy dinner.

Prep time: 10 minutes | Cooking time: 10 minutes | Servings: 2

Ingredients (0 points):

- 12 oz large shrimp, peeled and deveined
- 1 cup bell peppers, sliced (any color)
- 1 cup snow peas, trimmed
- 1/2 cup onion, sliced
- 2 cloves garlic, minced
- 1 tablespoon fresh ginger, minced
- 2 tablespoons soy sauce (low-sodium)
- 1 tablespoon rice vinegar
- 1/4 teaspoon red pepper flakes (optional, for spice)
- Cooking spray or a small amount of water for stir-frying

Step-by-Step Directions:

1. Prepare the Ingredients (0 points): I begin by peeling and deveining the shrimp if they aren't already prepared. I then slice the bell peppers, trim the snow peas, and slice the onion. I also mince the garlic and ginger.
2. Heat the Pan: In a large non-stick skillet or wok, I lightly spray cooking spray or add a small amount of water and heat it over medium-high heat.
3. Cook the Shrimp: Once the pan is hot, I add the shrimp to the skillet. I cook the shrimp for about 2-3 minutes on each side, or until they turn pink and opaque. I then remove the shrimp from the skillet and set them aside.
4. Stir-Fry the Vegetables: In the same skillet, I add the minced garlic and ginger, sautéing them for about 30 seconds until fragrant. I then add the sliced bell peppers, snow peas, and onions to the skillet. I stir-fry the vegetables for about 4-5 minutes, or until they are tender-crisp.
5. Combine and Season: I return the cooked shrimp to the skillet with the vegetables. I add the soy sauce, rice vinegar, and red pepper flakes (if using), tossing everything together to coat the shrimp and vegetables evenly with the sauce. I cook for an additional 1-2 minutes to allow the flavors to meld.
6. Serve: I divide the shrimp and vegetable stir-fry between two plates. The dish is ready to enjoy immediately, offering a delicious, nutritious, and satisfying meal.

Tips:

1. Add Extra Veggies: I can add other zero-point vegetables like mushrooms, zucchini, or bok choy to the stir-fry for added variety.
2. Make it Spicy: For more heat, I can increase the amount of red pepper flakes or add a dash of hot sauce.
3. Garnish with Fresh Herbs: For extra flavor, I can garnish the stir-fry with fresh cilantro or green onions before serving.

Nutritional Information:

- Calories: 190, Protein: 30g, Fat: 1g, Carbohydrates: 14g, Fiber: 4g, Sugar: 6g, Points: 0

Serving Suggestions:

1. Pair with Cauliflower Rice: I like to serve this stir-fry over cauliflower rice for a more filling meal that keeps the entire dish at zero points.
2. Serve with a Side Salad: A light side salad with a simple vinaigrette complements the flavors of the stir-fry and adds more fresh vegetables to the meal.

Grilled Salmon with a Side of Asparagus and Cherry Tomatoes

This Grilled Salmon with a Side of Asparagus and Cherry Tomatoes is a delicious, protein-packed dinner that's both light and satisfying. Salmon is rich in omega-3 fatty acids, making it a heart-healthy choice, while the asparagus and cherry tomatoes add a burst of fresh flavor and color. This meal is quick to prepare, nutritious, and perfectly fits within the Zero Point Weight Loss program.

Prep time: 10 minutes | Cooking time: 15 minutes | Servings: 2

Ingredients (0 points):

- 2 salmon fillets (about 4 oz each)
- 1 bunch asparagus, trimmed
- 1 cup cherry tomatoes, halved
- 2 cloves garlic, minced
- 1 tablespoon fresh lemon juice
- 1 tablespoon fresh parsley, chopped
- Salt and pepper to taste
- Cooking spray or a small amount of water for grilling and roasting

Step-by-Step Directions:

1. Prepare the Salmon: I start by seasoning the salmon fillets with salt, pepper, and a squeeze of fresh lemon juice. I then preheat my grill or grill pan over medium-high heat.
2. Grill the Salmon: I lightly spray the grill with cooking spray to prevent sticking. I place the salmon fillets on the grill, skin-side down (if the skin is on). I grill the salmon for about 4-5 minutes per side, depending on the thickness, until the fish is cooked through and easily flakes with a fork. Once done, I remove the salmon from the grill and let it rest for a minute.
3. Roast the Vegetables: While the salmon is grilling, I prepare the asparagus and cherry tomatoes. I preheat my oven to 400°F (200°C). I place the asparagus and halved cherry tomatoes on a baking sheet, drizzle them with a little fresh lemon juice, and season with minced garlic, salt, and pepper. I toss the vegetables to coat them evenly. I roast the vegetables in the preheated oven for about 10-12 minutes, or until the asparagus is tender and the cherry tomatoes are slightly blistered.
4. Serve: I divide the grilled salmon fillets between two plates. I then add the roasted asparagus and cherry tomatoes to each plate, garnishing the dish with chopped fresh parsley. The meal is ready to enjoy immediately, offering a nutritious, flavorful dinner.

Tips:

1. Add Extra Flavor: I can sprinkle some lemon zest over the salmon before grilling for an extra burst of citrus flavor.
2. Make it Spicy: If I enjoy a bit of heat, I can add a pinch of red pepper flakes to the asparagus and tomatoes before roasting.
3. Cook to Preference: For more well-done salmon, I can grill the fish a little longer, but I'll be careful not to overcook it to maintain its moisture and tenderness.

Nutritional Information:

- Calories: 250, Protein: 28g, Fat: 12g, Carbohydrates: 8g, Fiber: 4g, Sugar: 4g, Points: 0

Serving Suggestions:

1. Pair with a Light Salad: I like to serve this dish with a simple side salad of mixed greens dressed with lemon juice or a light vinaigrette for a refreshing complement.
2. Add a Grain (Optional): For a more filling meal, I can serve this dish with a side of quinoa or brown rice, though I'll need to count the points for the grains.

Turkey Meatballs in a Homemade Marinara Sauce with Spaghetti Squash

This recipe is a delicious, comforting dinner option that's both filling and healthy. The turkey meatballs are seasoned to perfection and paired with a rich, homemade marinara sauce. Serving them over spaghetti squash provides the satisfying texture of pasta without the carbs, making this meal ideal for staying on track with Weight Loss.

Prep time: 20 minutes | Cooking time: 40 minutes | Servings: 2

Ingredients (0 points):

- For the Turkey Meatballs:
- 8 oz lean ground turkey (99% fat-free)
- 1/4 cup onion, finely chopped
- 1 clove garlic, minced
- 1 tablespoon fresh parsley, chopped
- 1 teaspoon dried oregano
- 1/2 teaspoon dried basil
- Salt and pepper to taste
- For the Marinara Sauce:
- 1 can (15 oz) crushed tomatoes
- 1/2 cup onion, finely chopped
- 2 cloves garlic, minced
- 1 teaspoon dried oregano
- 1 teaspoon dried basil
- 1/4 teaspoon red pepper flakes (optional)
- Salt and pepper to taste
- Cooking spray or a small amount of water for sautéing
- For the Spaghetti Squash:
- 1 medium spaghetti squash)
- Salt and pepper to taste

Step-by-Step Directions:

1. Prepare the Spaghetti Squash: I start by preheating my oven to 400°F (200°C). I cut the spaghetti squash in half lengthwise and scoop out the seeds. I lightly season the inside with salt and pepper. I place the squash halves cut-side down on a baking sheet and roast them in the preheated oven for about 35-40 minutes, or until the flesh is tender and can be easily scraped into strands with a fork. Once done, I set the squash aside.
2. Make the Turkey Meatballs: While the squash is roasting, I prepare the turkey meatballs. In a mixing bowl, I combine the ground turkey, finely chopped onion, minced garlic, fresh parsley, dried oregano, dried basil, salt, and pepper. I mix everything together until well combined, then form the mixture into small meatballs, about 1 inch in diameter. In a non-stick skillet, I lightly spray cooking spray and heat it over medium heat. I add the meatballs to the skillet and cook them for about 8-10 minutes, turning occasionally, until they are browned on all sides and cooked through.
3. Make the Marinara Sauce: In the same skillet (after removing the meatballs), I add a bit more cooking spray or water if needed. I sauté the finely chopped onion and minced garlic over medium heat for about 3-4 minutes until softened. I then add the crushed tomatoes, dried oregano, dried basil, red pepper flakes (if using), salt, and pepper. I stir everything together and let the sauce simmer for about 15 minutes, allowing the flavors to meld together. I return the cooked meatballs to the skillet with the marinara sauce, gently stirring to coat the meatballs with the sauce. I let the meatballs simmer in the sauce for another 5 minutes.
4. Prepare the Spaghetti Squash: Once the spaghetti squash is cool enough to handle, I use a fork to scrape the flesh into spaghetti-like strands. I divide the strands between two plates.
5. Serve: I top the spaghetti squash with the turkey meatballs and marinara sauce. The dish is ready to enjoy immediately, offering a hearty, flavorful meal.

Tips:

1. Make it Cheesy (Optional): For a richer flavor, I can sprinkle a small amount of grated Parmesan cheese over the dish, but I'll need to count the points for the cheese.

Nutritional Information:

- Calories: 250, Protein: 30g, Fat: 4g, Carbohydrates: 20g, Fiber: 5g, Sugar: 8g, Points: 0

Grilled Portobello Mushrooms Stuffed with Spinach and Tomatoes

This Grilled Portobello Mushrooms Stuffed with Spinach and Tomatoes recipe is a flavorful and satisfying dinner option that's both healthy and delicious. The meaty texture of Portobello mushrooms makes them a perfect substitute for more calorie-dense foods, while the spinach and tomato stuffing adds a burst of freshness and nutrients. This dish is not only low in calories but also fits seamlessly into the Zero Point Weight Loss program, making it an excellent choice for a light yet fulfilling dinner.

Prep time: 10 minutes | Cooking time: 15 minutes | Servings: 2

Ingredients (0 points):

- 4 large Portobello mushrooms, stems removed and gills scraped out
- 4 cups fresh spinach, chopped
- 1 cup cherry tomatoes, halved
- 1 clove garlic, minced
- 1 tablespoon fresh basil, chopped
- 1 tablespoon balsamic vinegar
- Salt and pepper to taste
- Cooking spray or a small amount of water for sautéing and grilling

Step-by-Step Directions:

1. Prepare the Mushrooms: I start by cleaning the Portobello mushrooms, removing the stems, and scraping out the gills with a spoon. This will create space for the stuffing and allow the mushrooms to cook more evenly.
2. Cook the Spinach Filling: In a large non-stick skillet, I lightly spray cooking spray or add a small amount of water and heat it over medium heat. I add the minced garlic and sauté it for about 30 seconds until fragrant. I then add the chopped spinach to the skillet, cooking it for 2-3 minutes until it's wilted. I season the spinach with a pinch of salt and pepper. After the spinach is wilted, I stir in the halved cherry tomatoes and cook for another 2 minutes, just until the tomatoes are slightly softened. I remove the skillet from the heat and stir in the chopped basil.
3. Grill the Mushrooms: I preheat my grill or grill pan over medium-high heat. I lightly spray the mushrooms with cooking spray and season them with salt and pepper on both sides. I place the mushrooms on the grill, gill-side down, and cook them for about 4-5 minutes on each side until they are tender and have nice grill marks.
4. Stuff the Mushrooms: Once the mushrooms are grilled, I carefully spoon the spinach and tomato mixture into each mushroom cap, dividing the filling evenly between the four mushrooms.
5. Finish with Balsamic Vinegar: I drizzle the stuffed mushrooms with balsamic vinegar, which adds a tangy sweetness that complements the earthy flavors of the mushrooms and the freshness of the spinach and tomatoes.
6. Serve: I serve the grilled Portobello mushrooms immediately, while they are still warm. This dish is light, flavorful, and perfect for a nutritious dinner.

Tips:

1. Add Cheese (Optional): For a richer flavor, I can sprinkle a small amount of grated Parmesan or mozzarella cheese over the stuffed mushrooms before serving, but I'll need to count the points for the cheese.
2. Customize the Filling: I can add other zero-point vegetables like onions, bell peppers, or zucchini to the spinach filling for added variety.
3. Use Fresh Herbs: Fresh basil adds a bright, fresh flavor, but I can also use other herbs like thyme or parsley depending on my preference.

Nutritional Information:

- Calories: 120, Protein: 6g, Fat: 2g, Carbohydrates: 20g, Fiber: 6g, Sugar: 9g, Points: 0

Pan-Seared Tilapia with a Cucumber and Tomato Salad

This Pan-Seared Tilapia with a Cucumber and Tomato Salad is a light, refreshing, and satisfying dinner that's perfect for keeping me on track with my weight loss goals. The tilapia is seared to perfection, providing a delicate, flaky texture, while the cucumber and tomato salad adds a fresh, crunchy element that complements the fish. This meal is quick to prepare, full of nutrients, and fits seamlessly into the Zero Point Weight Loss program.

Prep time: 10 minutes | Cooking time: 10 minutes | Servings: 2

Ingredients (0 points):

- For the Tilapia:
- 2 tilapia fillets (about 4 oz each)
- 1 clove garlic, minced
- 1 tablespoon fresh lemon juice
- 1 teaspoon paprika
- Salt and pepper to taste
- Cooking spray or a small amount of water for searing

- For the Cucumber and Tomato Salad:
- 1 cup cucumber, sliced
- 1 cup cherry tomatoes, halved
- 1/4 cup red onion, thinly sliced
- 1 tablespoon fresh parsley, chopped
- 1 tablespoon fresh lemon juice
- Salt and pepper to taste

Step-by-Step Directions:

1. Prepare the Tilapia: I start by seasoning the tilapia fillets with salt, pepper, paprika, and a squeeze of fresh lemon juice. I also rub the minced garlic onto the fillets for added flavor.
2. I then preheat a non-stick skillet over medium-high heat and lightly spray it with cooking spray to prevent sticking.
3. Pan-Sear the Tilapia: Once the skillet is hot, I place the tilapia fillets in the pan. I cook the fillets for about 3-4 minutes on each side, or until the fish is opaque and flakes easily with a fork. I then remove the tilapia from the pan and let it rest for a minute while I prepare the salad.
4. Prepare the Cucumber and Tomato Salad: In a large mixing bowl, I combine the sliced cucumber, halved cherry tomatoes, thinly sliced red onion, and chopped parsley. I drizzle the salad with fresh lemon juice and season it with a pinch of salt and pepper. I gently toss the salad to ensure that all the ingredients are evenly coated with the lemon juice and seasoning.
5. Serve: I divide the cucumber and tomato salad between two plates, placing a tilapia fillet on each plate. The dish is ready to enjoy immediately, offering a fresh, flavorful, and healthy meal.

Tips:

1. If I want a bit more flavor, I can add a sprinkle of dried oregano or thyme to the tilapia before cooking.
2. Make it Spicy: For a touch of heat, I can add a pinch of red pepper flakes to the tilapia or the salad.
3. Use Fresh Herbs: Fresh parsley adds a bright, fresh flavor, but I can also use other herbs like dill or basil depending on my preference.

Nutritional Information:

- Calories: 180, Protein: 30g, Fat: 2g, Carbohydrates: 8g, Fiber: 2g, Sugar: 4g, Points: 0

Serving Suggestions:

1. Pair with a Side of Steamed Vegetables: I like to serve this dish with a side of steamed asparagus or green beans to keep the meal light and nutritious.
2. Add a Grain (Optional): For a more filling meal, I can serve this dish with a side of quinoa or brown rice, though I'll need to count the points for the grains.

Baked Chicken Breast with Cauliflower Mash and Steamed Green Beans

This Baked Chicken Breast with Cauliflower Mash and Steamed Green Beans is a classic, comforting dinner that's both nutritious and satisfying. The chicken breast is baked to juicy perfection, while the cauliflower mash serves as a creamy, low-carb alternative to traditional mashed potatoes. Paired with steamed green beans, this meal is both balanced and filling, making it an ideal choice for the Zero Point Weight Loss program.

Prep time: 15 minutes | Cooking time: 30 minutes | Servings: 2

Ingredients (0 points):

- For the Baked Chicken Breast:
- 2 boneless, skinless chicken breasts (about 4 oz each)
- 1 tablespoon fresh lemon juice
- 1 teaspoon garlic powder
- 1 teaspoon dried thyme
- Salt and pepper to taste
- Cooking spray or a small amount of water for baking

- For the Cauliflower Mash:
- 1 medium head of cauliflower, cut into florets
- 1 clove garlic, minced
- 1 tablespoon fresh parsley, chopped
- Salt and pepper to taste
- For the Steamed Green Beans:
- 2 cups fresh green beans, trimmed
- Salt and pepper to taste

Step-by-Step Directions:

1. Preheat the Oven: I begin by preheating my oven to 375°F (190°C). While the oven is heating, I prepare the chicken breasts.
2. Prepare the Chicken Breasts: I season the chicken breasts with fresh lemon juice, garlic powder, dried thyme, salt, and pepper. I then place the seasoned chicken breasts in a baking dish lightly sprayed with cooking spray. I bake the chicken in the preheated oven for about 25-30 minutes, or until the chicken is cooked through and reaches an internal temperature of 165°F (75°C). Once done, I remove the chicken from the oven and let it rest for a few minutes.
3. Prepare the Cauliflower Mash: While the chicken is baking, I steam the cauliflower florets until they are tender, about 10-12 minutes. I drain the cauliflower and transfer it to a food processor.
4. I add the minced garlic, chopped parsley, salt, and pepper to the cauliflower, then blend until the mixture is smooth and creamy. If I prefer a chunkier texture, I can mash the cauliflower by hand using a potato masher.
5. Steam the Green Beans: In the last 10 minutes of the chicken's cooking time, I steam the green beans in a steamer basket over boiling water. I steam them for about 5-7 minutes until they are tender but still crisp. I then season the green beans with a pinch of salt and pepper.
6. Serve: I divide the cauliflower mash and steamed green beans between two plates. I then place a baked chicken breast on each plate. The dish is ready to enjoy immediately, offering a balanced and satisfying meal.

Tips:

1. I can add a pinch of smoked paprika or rosemary to the chicken seasoning for a different flavor profile.
2. Make the Mash Creamier: For an even creamier mash, I can add a small amount of unsweetened almond milk, but I'll need to count the points for any added ingredients.
3. Roast the Green Beans (Optional): For a different texture, I can toss the green beans with a little lemon juice and roast them in the oven alongside the chicken.

Nutritional Information:

- Calories: 220, Protein: 35g, Fat: 4g, Carbohydrates: 16g, Fiber: 7g, Sugar: 5g, Points: 0

Stuffed Bell Peppers with Ground Turkey and Diced Vegetables

These Stuffed Bell Peppers with Ground Turkey and Diced Vegetables are a delicious and satisfying dinner option that's both hearty and healthy. The bell peppers are stuffed with a flavorful mixture of lean ground turkey and a variety of diced vegetables, creating a balanced meal that's both filling and low in calories. This dish is not only tasty but also fits perfectly into the Zero Point Weight Loss program, making it a great choice for a nutritious dinner.

Prep time: 15 minutes | Cooking time: 35 minutes | Servings: 2

Ingredients (0 points):

- 2 large bell peppers (any color), tops cut off and seeds removed (0 points)
- 8 oz lean ground turkey (99% fat-free)
- 1/2 cup onion, finely chopped
- 1/2 cup zucchini, diced
- 1/2 cup carrots, diced
- 1/2 cup mushrooms, diced
- 1 clove garlic, minced
- 1 teaspoon dried oregano
- 1 teaspoon dried basil
- 1/4 teaspoon red pepper flakes (optional, for spice)
- Salt and pepper to taste
- Cooking spray or a small amount of water for sautéing

Step-by-Step Directions:

1. Preheat the Oven: I start by preheating my oven to 375°F (190°C). While the oven is heating, I prepare the bell peppers and the stuffing mixture.
2. Prepare the Bell Peppers: I cut the tops off the bell peppers and remove the seeds and membranes from inside. I then place the hollowed-out peppers in a baking dish.
3. Cook the Filling: In a large non-stick skillet, I lightly spray cooking spray or add a small amount of water and heat it over medium heat. I add the minced garlic and chopped onion to the skillet and sauté them for about 2-3 minutes until the onion is softened. I then add the ground turkey to the skillet, cooking it for about 5-7 minutes, or until it's browned and cooked through. I use a spoon to break up the turkey into small pieces as it cooks. Once the turkey is cooked, I add the diced zucchini, carrots, and mushrooms to the skillet. I stir in the dried oregano, dried basil, red pepper flakes (if using), salt, and pepper. I cook the mixture for another 5 minutes, until the vegetables are tender.
4. Stuff the Peppers:I carefully spoon the turkey and vegetable mixture into the hollowed-out bell peppers, filling them evenly. I gently press the filling down to pack it in well.
5. Bake the Stuffed Peppers: I cover the baking dish with foil and bake the stuffed peppers in the preheated oven for about 30 minutes. After 30 minutes, I remove the foil and bake for an additional 5 minutes to allow the tops of the peppers to brown slightly.
6. Serve: I remove the stuffed peppers from the oven and let them cool slightly before serving. Each pepper is served as a complete meal, providing a nutritious, flavorful dinner that's ready to enjoy.

Tips:

1. I can sprinkle a little fresh parsley or basil on top of the peppers before serving for added freshness.
2. Make it Cheesy (Optional): If I want to add a bit of richness, I can sprinkle a small amount of grated Parmesan or mozzarella cheese over the top of the peppers during the last 5 minutes of baking, but I'll need to count the points for the cheese.
3. Use Different Vegetables: I can customize the filling by using other zero-point vegetables like spinach, tomatoes, or bell peppers.

Nutritional Information:

- Calories: 220, Protein: 28g, Fat: 4g, Carbohydrates: 20g, Fiber: 7g, Sugar: 10g, Points: 0

Grilled Tuna Steak with a Side of Roasted Zucchini and Squash

This Grilled Tuna Steak with a Side of Roasted Zucchini and Squash is a light, flavorful dinner option that's perfect for keeping me on track with my weight loss goals. Tuna steaks are packed with protein and have a deliciously firm texture that pairs beautifully with the roasted zucchini and squash. This meal is easy to prepare, full of fresh flavors, and fits seamlessly into the Zero Point Weight Loss program.

Prep time: 10 minutes | Cooking time: 20 minutes | Servings: 2

Ingredients (0 points):

- For the Grilled Tuna Steak:
- 2 tuna steaks (about 5-6 oz each)
- 1 tablespoon fresh lemon juice
- 1 clove garlic, minced
- 1 teaspoon dried thyme
- 1/2 teaspoon black pepper
- Salt to taste
- Cooking spray or a small amount of water for grilling

- For the Roasted Zucchini and Squash:
- 1 medium zucchini, sliced into rounds
- 1 medium yellow squash, sliced into rounds
- 1 teaspoon dried oregano
- 1 clove garlic, minced
- Salt and pepper to taste
- Cooking spray or a small amount of water for roasting

Step-by-Step Directions:

1. Preheat the Grill and Oven: I start by preheating my grill to medium-high heat and my oven to 400°F (200°C).
2. Prepare the Tuna Steaks: While the grill is heating, I marinate the tuna steaks. I rub the tuna steaks with fresh lemon juice, minced garlic, dried thyme, black pepper, and a pinch of salt. I let the steaks sit for about 10 minutes to allow the flavors to meld.
3. Prepare the Zucchini and Squash: I slice the zucchini and yellow squash into rounds and place them in a mixing bowl. I toss them with minced garlic, dried oregano, salt, and pepper until evenly coated. I spread the zucchini and squash slices in a single layer on a baking sheet, lightly sprayed with cooking spray. I roast the vegetables in the preheated oven for about 15-20 minutes, or until they are tender and slightly browned.
4. Grill the Tuna Steaks: While the vegetables are roasting, I grill the tuna steaks. I lightly spray the grill with cooking spray to prevent sticking. I place the tuna steaks on the hot grill and cook them for about 3-4 minutes per side for medium-rare, or longer if I prefer the tuna more well-done. The steaks should be firm but still tender.
5. Serve: I divide the roasted zucchini and squash between two plates and place a grilled tuna steak on each plate. The dish is ready to enjoy immediately, offering a nutritious and satisfying dinner.

Tips:

1. Add Extra Flavor: For a more robust flavor, I can add a pinch of smoked paprika or red pepper flakes to the tuna marinade.
2. Tuna can dry out quickly, so I make sure to grill it just until it reaches my desired doneness.
3. If I have fresh thyme or oregano on hand, I can use them in place of dried herbs for a more vibrant flavor.

Nutritional Information:

- Calories: 250, Protein: 42g, Fat: 5g, Carbohydrates: 10g, Fiber: 3g, Sugar: 5g, Points: 0

Serving Suggestions:

1. Pair with a Side Salad: I like to serve this dish with a light side salad of mixed greens dressed with a lemon vinaigrette to keep the meal fresh and balanced.

Turkey and Cabbage Rolls with a Tomato-Based Sauce

These Turkey and Cabbage Rolls with a Tomato-Based Sauce are a hearty and satisfying dinner option that's both healthy and delicious. The rolls are made with lean ground turkey and wrapped in tender cabbage leaves, then baked in a flavorful tomato sauce. This dish is low in calories but full of flavor, making it a perfect choice for the Zero Point Weight Loss program.

Prep time: 20 minutes | Cooking time: 45 minutes | Servings: 2

Ingredients (0 points):

- For the Cabbage Rolls:
- 8 large cabbage leaves
- 8 oz lean ground turkey (99% fat-free)
- 1/2 cup onion, finely chopped
- 1/2 cup carrots, grated
- 1/2 cup mushrooms, finely chopped
- 1 clove garlic, minced
- 1 tablespoon fresh parsley, chopped
- 1 teaspoon dried oregano
- Salt and pepper to taste
- Cooking spray or a small amount of water for sautéing
- For the Tomato-Based Sauce:
- 1 can (15 oz) crushed tomatoes
- 1/2 cup onion, finely chopped
- 1 clove garlic, minced
- 1 teaspoon dried basil
- 1 teaspoon dried oregano
- Salt and pepper to taste
- 1/4 teaspoon red pepper flakes (optional, for spice)

Step-by-Step Directions:

1. Prepare the Cabbage Leaves: I start by bringing a large pot of water to a boil. Once boiling, I carefully add the cabbage leaves and blanch them for 2-3 minutes until they are pliable. I then remove the leaves from the water and set them aside to cool.
2. Prepare the Filling: In a large non-stick skillet, I lightly spray cooking spray or add a small amount of water and heat it over medium heat. I add the minced garlic and chopped onion, sautéing them for about 2-3 minutes until the onion is softened. I then add the ground turkey, grated carrots, and chopped mushrooms to the skillet, cooking the mixture for about 5-7 minutes until the turkey is fully cooked. I season the filling with dried oregano, salt, and pepper, then stir in the chopped parsley.
3. Make the Tomato-Based Sauce: In a separate saucepan, I prepare the tomato sauce. I lightly spray the pan with cooking spray and sauté the minced garlic and chopped onion over medium heat for about 3 minutes until softened. I add the crushed tomatoes, dried basil, dried oregano, salt, pepper, and red pepper flakes (if using). I stir the sauce and let it simmer for about 10 minutes to allow the flavors to meld together.
4. Assemble the Cabbage Rolls: I lay each cabbage leaf flat and spoon a portion of the turkey mixture into the center of the leaf. I fold the sides of the leaf over the filling and then roll it up tightly to create a neat roll. I place each rolled cabbage leaf seam-side down in a baking dish.
5. Bake the Cabbage Rolls: I pour the tomato-based sauce over the cabbage rolls, ensuring they are fully covered. I cover the baking dish with foil and bake the rolls in a preheated oven at 375°F (190°C) for about 35-40 minutes, or until the rolls are heated through and the flavors have melded.
6. Serve: I remove the cabbage rolls from the oven and let them cool slightly before serving. I divide the rolls between two plates, spooning extra sauce over the top for added flavor.

Tips:

1. I can mix in other zero-point vegetables like bell peppers or zucchini to the filling for added flavor.

Nutritional Information:

- Calories: 220, Protein: 30g, Fat: 4g, Carbohydrates: 20g, Fiber: 6g, Sugar: 8g, Points: 0

Herb-Roasted Chicken Thighs with a Side of Sautéed Spinach and Garlic

This Herb-Roasted Chicken Thighs with a Side of Sautéed Spinach and Garlic is a flavorful and satisfying dinner option that's perfect for a healthy, zero-point meal. The chicken thighs are seasoned with a mix of fresh herbs and roasted to crispy perfection, while the sautéed spinach with garlic adds a nutritious and delicious side. This meal is simple to prepare, yet it's packed with flavor and nutrients, making it an excellent choice for the Weight Loss.

Prep time: 10 minutes | Cooking time: 30 minutes | Servings: 2

Ingredients (0 points):

- For the Herb-Roasted Chicken Thighs:
- 4 skinless, boneless chicken thighs
- 1 tablespoon fresh rosemary, chopped
- 1 tablespoon fresh thyme, chopped
- 2 cloves garlic, minced
- 1 tablespoon fresh lemon juice
- Salt and pepper to taste
- Cooking spray or a small amount of water for roasting
- For the Sautéed Spinach and Garlic:
- 4 cups fresh spinach, washed and dried
- 2 cloves garlic, minced
- 1 teaspoon olive oil (optional, but use only a small amount to keep points low)
- Salt and pepper to taste

Step-by-Step Directions:

1. Preheat the Oven: I start by preheating my oven to 400°F (200°C). While the oven is heating, I prepare the chicken thighs.
2. Prepare the Chicken Thighs: I season the chicken thighs with fresh rosemary, thyme, minced garlic, fresh lemon juice, salt, and pepper. I ensure the thighs are evenly coated with the herbs and seasoning. I lightly spray a baking dish with cooking spray and place the seasoned chicken thighs in the dish.
3. Roast the Chicken Thighs: I roast the chicken thighs in the preheated oven for about 25-30 minutes, or until the chicken is cooked through and reaches an internal temperature of 165°F (75°C). The thighs should be golden brown and slightly crispy on the outside.
4. Prepare the Sautéed Spinach: While the chicken is roasting, I heat a non-stick skillet over medium heat. I add the minced garlic and sauté it for about 30 seconds until it becomes fragrant. I then add the fresh spinach to the skillet, stirring occasionally until the spinach is wilted, about 3-4 minutes. I season the spinach with a pinch of salt and pepper to taste. If I choose to use a tiny amount of olive oil, I add it at this stage, but it's not necessary to keep the points at zero.
5. Serve: I divide the sautéed spinach between two plates and place two herb-roasted chicken thighs on each plate. The dish is ready to enjoy immediately, offering a flavorful and nutritious meal.

Tips:

1. Add Extra Flavor: For a bit more zest, I can add lemon zest to the chicken seasoning or drizzle additional lemon juice over the chicken before serving.
2. If I prefer other herbs, I can substitute or add fresh parsley, basil, or oregano to the chicken seasoning.
3. If I enjoy a bit of heat, I can add a pinch of red pepper flakes to the spinach while it's sautéing.

Nutritional Information:

- Calories: 240, Protein: 30g, Fat: 10g, Carbohydrates: 6g, Fiber: 4g, Sugar: 1g, Points: 0

Serving Suggestions:

1. Pair with a Side Salad: I like to serve this dish with a simple green salad dressed with lemon juice or a light vinaigrette to keep the meal fresh and balanced.
2. Add a Grain (Optional): For a more filling meal, I can serve this dish with a side of quinoa or brown rice, though I'll need to count the points for the grains.

Slow-Cooked Beef Stew with Carrots, Celery, and Onions

This Slow-Cooked Beef Stew with Carrots, Celery, and Onions is a comforting and hearty dinner option that's perfect for chilly evenings. The stew is made with lean beef, which is slow-cooked until tender, and packed with nutritious vegetables like carrots, celery, and onions. The flavors meld together beautifully over the long cooking time, creating a rich and satisfying meal that fits seamlessly into the Zero Point Weight Loss program.

Prep time: 15 minutes | Cooking time: 6-8 hours on low or 4-5 hours on high | Servings: 2

Ingredients (0 points):

- 12 oz lean beef stew meat, trimmed of visible fat
- 2 cups carrots, sliced
- 2 cups celery, sliced
- 1 large onion, chopped
- 2 cloves garlic, minced
- 2 cups low-sodium beef broth
- 1 tablespoon tomato paste
- 1 teaspoon dried thyme
- 1 teaspoon dried rosemary
- 1 bay leaf
- Salt and pepper to taste
- Cooking spray or a small amount of water for searing

Step-by-Step Directions:

1. Prepare the Ingredients: I begin by trimming any visible fat from the beef stew meat to keep it lean. I then chop the carrots, celery, and onion, and mince the garlic.
2. Sear the Beef (Optional): While this step is optional, it adds a deeper flavor to the stew. I lightly spray a large skillet with cooking spray and heat it over medium-high heat. I sear the beef on all sides until it's browned, about 4-5 minutes. Once browned, I transfer the beef to the slow cooker.
3. Assemble the Stew: In the slow cooker, I add the sliced carrots, celery, chopped onion, and minced garlic. I then add the seared beef, low-sodium beef broth, tomato paste, dried thyme, dried rosemary, and bay leaf. I season with salt and pepper to taste. I stir everything together to ensure the beef and vegetables are evenly distributed and covered with the broth.
4. Slow Cook the Stew: I cover the slow cooker with the lid and cook the stew on low for 6-8 hours or on high for 4-5 hours. The long cooking time allows the beef to become tender and the flavors to meld together beautifully.
5. Finish and Serve: Once the cooking time is complete, I check the seasoning and adjust if necessary. I remove the bay leaf before serving. I divide the stew between two bowls, ensuring each serving gets a generous portion of beef and vegetables.

Tips:

1. Thicken the Stew (Optional): If I prefer a thicker stew, I can remove the lid in the last 30 minutes of cooking to allow some of the liquid to evaporate or add a small amount of cornstarch mixed with water, though this may add points.
2. Add Extra Vegetables: I can easily add other zero-point vegetables like potatoes, green beans, or mushrooms to the stew for added flavor and nutrition.

Nutritional Information:

- Calories: 280, Protein: 36g, Fat: 6g, Carbohydrates: 20g, Fiber: 6g, Sugar: 8g, Points: 0

Serving Suggestions:

1. Pair with a Side Salad: I like to serve this hearty stew with a simple side salad of mixed greens dressed with lemon juice or a light vinaigrette for a refreshing contrast.
2. Serve with Whole Grain Bread (Optional): For a more filling meal, I can serve this stew with a slice of whole grain bread, though I'll need to count the points for the bread.

DESSERT RECIPES

Baked Cinnamon Apples with a Sprinkle of Nutmeg and Fresh Berries

This Baked Cinnamon Apples with a Sprinkle of Nutmeg and Fresh Berries recipe is a warm, comforting dessert or light dinner option that's perfect for satisfying my sweet cravings without straying from my weight loss goals. The apples are baked until tender and naturally sweet, while the cinnamon and nutmeg add a fragrant, warming spice. Paired with fresh berries, this dish is not only delicious but also fits perfectly into the Zero Point Weight Loss program.

Prep time: 10 minutes | Cooking time: 20-25 minutes | Servings: 2

Ingredients (0 points):

- 2 medium apples, cored and sliced
- 1 teaspoon ground cinnamon
- 1/4 teaspoon ground nutmeg
- 1/2 teaspoon vanilla extract
- 1 cup mixed fresh berries (e.g., strawberries, blueberries, raspberries)
- Cooking spray or a small amount of water for baking

Step-by-Step Directions:

1. I start by preheating my oven to 375°F (190°C). While the oven is heating, I prepare the apples.
2. Prepare the Apples: I core and slice the apples into thin wedges, leaving the skin on for added fiber and texture. In a mixing bowl, I toss the apple slices with ground cinnamon, ground nutmeg, and vanilla extract until the slices are evenly coated.
3. Bake the Apples: I lightly spray a baking dish with cooking spray to prevent sticking, then arrange the apple slices in a single layer in the dish. I cover the dish with foil and bake the apples in the preheated oven for about 20-25 minutes, or until they are tender and fragrant. Halfway through the baking time, I stir the apples gently to ensure even cooking.
4. Prepare the Berries: While the apples are baking, I rinse and prepare the fresh berries. I can use a mix of strawberries, blueberries, raspberries, or any berries I prefer.
5. Serve: Once the apples are baked, I remove them from the oven and let them cool slightly. I divide the baked apples between two plates and top each serving with a handful of fresh berries. This dish is best served warm, but it's also delicious at room temperature.

Tips:

1. Add a Crunch: For added texture, I can sprinkle a few crushed nuts (like almonds or walnuts) over the top, though I'll need to count the points for the nuts.
2. Make it Creamy (Optional): If I want a creamy element, I can add a dollop of fat-free Greek yogurt on top, but I'll need to check the points if using flavored yogurt.
3. Sweeten to Taste: The natural sweetness of the apples should be enough, but if I want it sweeter, I can add a few drops of a zero-calorie sweetener.

Nutritional Information:

- Calories: 120, Protein: 1g, Fat: 0g, Carbohydrates: 31g, Fiber: 7g, Sugar: 23g, Points: 0

Serving Suggestions:

1. I like to enjoy this dish with a cup of herbal tea or hot lemon water, making it a soothing end to my meal.
2. Add a Scoop of Frozen Berries (Optional): For a cool contrast, I can serve this dish with a scoop of frozen berries instead of fresh ones.

Fresh Fruit Salad with Pineapple, Mango, and Kiwi

This Fresh Fruit Salad with Pineapple, Mango, and Kiwi is a vibrant and refreshing dish that's perfect for a light dinner or a satisfying dessert. The combination of sweet pineapple, juicy mango, and tangy kiwi creates a delightful medley of flavors and textures. This salad is naturally sweet and packed with vitamins and nutrients, making it an ideal choice for the Zero Point Weight Loss program.

Prep time: 10 minutes | Cooking time: None | Servings: 2

Ingredients (0 points):

- 1 cup fresh pineapple, diced
- 1 cup fresh mango, diced
- 2 kiwis, peeled and sliced
- 1 tablespoon fresh lime juice
- 1 tablespoon fresh mint leaves, chopped (optional)

Step-by-Step Directions:

1. Prepare the Fruit: I begin by dicing the fresh pineapple and mango into bite-sized pieces. I then peel and slice the kiwis into rounds. If I prefer smaller pieces, I can dice the kiwi as well.
2. Assemble the Salad: In a large mixing bowl, I combine the diced pineapple, mango, and sliced kiwi. I drizzle the fresh lime juice over the fruit, which adds a zesty flavor and helps prevent the fruit from browning. I gently toss the fruit to ensure the lime juice is evenly distributed. If I'm using fresh mint, I sprinkle the chopped mint leaves over the top and give it another gentle toss.
3. Serve: I divide the fruit salad between two bowls, serving it immediately while the fruit is fresh and juicy. This salad is a light, refreshing option that's perfect for a warm evening or as a healthy dessert.

Tips:

1. Chill Before Serving: If I have time, I like to chill the fruit salad in the refrigerator for about 15-20 minutes before serving. This makes it even more refreshing, especially on a hot day.
2. Add Extra Fruit: I can easily add other zero-point fruits like berries, oranges, or melon to the salad for added variety and flavor.
3. Use Fresh Herbs: If I have fresh basil on hand, I can use it instead of mint for a different flavor profile.

Nutritional Information:

- Calories: 110, Protein: 1g, Fat: 0g, Carbohydrates: 28g, Fiber: 4g, Sugar: 23g, Points: 0

Serving Suggestions:

1. Pair with a Yogurt Dressing (Optional): For a creamier option, I can mix a little fat-free Greek yogurt with honey and drizzle it over the fruit salad, though I'll need to check the points for the yogurt.
2. Serve with a Light Snack: If I'm having this salad as a light dinner, I might pair it with a small handful of almonds or a boiled egg for added protein, though I'll need to account for the points.

Chilled Mixed Berry Compote with a Dollop of Fat-Free Greek Yogurt

This Chilled Mixed Berry Compote with a Dollop of Fat-Free Greek Yogurt is a light and refreshing dessert or dinner option that's both satisfying and nutritious. The mixed berries are gently simmered to release their natural juices, creating a sweet and tangy compote that pairs perfectly with the creamy Greek yogurt. This dish is simple to prepare and fits seamlessly into the Zero Point Weight Loss program.

Prep time: 5 minutes | Cooking time: 10 minutes Chill Time: 30 minutes (optional) | Servings: 2

Ingredients (0 points):

- 1 cup strawberries, hulled and sliced
- 1 cup blueberries
- 1 cup raspberries
- 1 teaspoon fresh lemon juice
- 1/2 teaspoon vanilla extract
- 1 cup fat-free Greek yogurt
- Fresh mint leaves for garnish (optional)

Step-by-Step Directions:

1. Prepare the Berries: I start by hulling and slicing the strawberries, then combine them with the blueberries and raspberries in a medium saucepan.
2. Cook the Compote: I add the fresh lemon juice and vanilla extract to the saucepan with the berries. I then cook the mixture over medium heat, stirring occasionally, until the berries start to break down and release their juices, about 8-10 minutes. Once the berries have softened and the juices have thickened slightly, I remove the saucepan from the heat. I let the compote cool to room temperature, then transfer it to the refrigerator to chill for at least 30 minutes if I prefer it cold.
3. Prepare the Yogurt: While the compote is chilling, I prepare the fat-free Greek yogurt by spooning it into two bowls.
4. Serve: I divide the chilled berry compote between the two bowls of Greek yogurt. I can garnish each serving with a sprig of fresh mint for a pop of color and added freshness.

Tips:

1. Adjust Sweetness: If I prefer a sweeter compote, I can add a few drops of a zero-calorie sweetener while cooking the berries, but this is usually unnecessary as the natural sweetness of the berries is sufficient.
2. Make It Fancy: For a more decadent presentation, I can layer the compote and yogurt in a clear glass, creating a parfait-style dessert.
3. Chill Overnight: If I want an even more pronounced flavor, I can prepare the compote the night before and let it chill overnight, allowing the flavors to meld together beautifully.

Nutritional Information:

- Calories: 110, Protein: 12g, Fat: 0g, Carbohydrates: 20g, Fiber: 5g, Sugar: 14g, Points: 0

Serving Suggestions:

1. Serve as Breakfast: This dish also makes a great breakfast, especially when paired with a sprinkle of zero-point granola or nuts for added texture, though I'll need to account for any additional points.
2. Pair with a Hot Beverage: I like to enjoy this compote with a cup of herbal tea or coffee, making it a comforting and balanced meal or dessert.

Grilled Peaches with a Drizzle of Balsamic Glaze

Grilled Peaches with a Drizzle of Balsamic Glaze is a delightful and elegant dessert or light dinner option that's perfect for summer. The natural sweetness of the peaches is enhanced by grilling, which caramelizes the sugars and adds a smoky flavor. The balsamic glaze adds a tangy contrast, creating a dish that's both simple and sophisticated. This recipe fits perfectly into the Zero Point Weight Loss program, allowing me to enjoy a sweet treat without worrying about added calories.

Prep time: 5 minutes | Cooking time: 8 minutes | Servings: 2

Ingredients (0 points):

- 2 ripe peaches, halved and pitted
- 1 tablespoon balsamic vinegar
- 1 teaspoon honey or maple syrup (optional, to taste) (0 points)
- Fresh mint leaves for garnish (optional)

Step-by-Step Directions:

1. Preheat the Grill: I start by preheating my grill or grill pan to medium-high heat. While the grill is heating, I prepare the peaches.
2. Prepare the Peaches: I wash the peaches, cut them in half, and remove the pits. If the peaches are very firm, I can score the cut side lightly with a knife to help them cook evenly.
3. Grill the Peaches: I place the peach halves on the grill, cut side down. I grill them for about 3-4 minutes on each side, or until they have nice grill marks and are slightly softened. The grilling time can vary depending on the ripeness of the peaches, so I keep an eye on them to prevent overcooking.
4. Make the Balsamic Glaze: While the peaches are grilling, I prepare the balsamic glaze. I pour the balsamic vinegar into a small saucepan and bring it to a simmer over medium heat. I cook the vinegar for about 5 minutes, or until it reduces by half and becomes slightly thickened.
5. If I prefer a sweeter glaze, I can stir in a teaspoon of honey or maple syrup at this point, but this is optional and does not add any points.
6. Serve: Once the peaches are grilled to perfection, I remove them from the grill and place them on two plates, cut side up. I drizzle the warm balsamic glaze over the peaches. For an extra touch of freshness, I can garnish the dish with a few fresh mint leaves.

Tips:

1. Choose Ripe Peaches: I make sure to select peaches that are ripe but still firm to the touch. Overripe peaches may become too soft on the grill.
2. Add a Creamy Element (Optional): For a more indulgent dessert, I can add a dollop of fat-free Greek yogurt or a scoop of sugar-free vanilla ice cream, though I'll need to check the points for any additional toppings.
3. Use Different Fruits: This recipe also works well with other stone fruits like nectarines or plums if I want to switch things up.

Nutritional Information:

- Calories: 80, Protein: 1g, Fat: 0g, Carbohydrates: 21g, Fiber: 3g, Sugar: 18g, Points: 0

Serving Suggestions:

1. Pair with a Light Salad: I like to serve these grilled peaches as a sweet complement to a savory salad, such as arugula with a light lemon vinaigrette.
2. Serve with Nuts (Optional): For a bit of crunch, I can sprinkle some toasted almonds or walnuts over the peaches, but I'll need to account for the points.

Frozen Banana and Strawberry "Nice Cream"

Frozen Banana and Strawberry "Nice Cream" is a refreshing and guilt-free dessert that's perfect for satisfying my sweet tooth without derailing my weight loss goals. Made simply by blending frozen bananas and strawberries, this creamy treat mimics the texture of ice cream but is entirely free from added sugars and dairy. It's a quick and easy recipe that fits perfectly into the Zero Point Weight Loss program.

Prep time: 5 minutes (plus freezing time for bananas)| Cooking time: None | Servings: 2

Ingredients (0 points):

- 2 ripe bananas, sliced and frozen (0 points)
- 1 cup strawberries, hulled and frozen (0 points)

Step-by-Step Directions:

1. Prepare the Ingredients (0 points): Before making the nice cream, I need to peel and slice the bananas, then place them in the freezer for at least 2 hours or until they are fully frozen. I also hull the strawberries and freeze them along with the bananas.
2. Blend the Nice Cream: Once the bananas and strawberries are frozen solid, I transfer them to a high-powered blender or food processor. I blend the fruit on high until it reaches a smooth and creamy consistency. If needed, I can stop the blender occasionally to scrape down the sides and ensure everything is evenly blended.
3. Serve Immediately: I divide the nice cream between two bowls and serve it immediately. The texture is best enjoyed fresh, as it's creamy and soft like traditional soft-serve ice cream.

Tips:

1. Add a Splash of Liquid: If the nice cream is too thick to blend, I can add a small splash of water, unsweetened almond milk, or any other zero-point liquid to help it along.
2. Enhance the Flavor: For added flavor, I can blend in a dash of vanilla extract or a pinch of cinnamon.
3. Make it Chunky: If I prefer some texture, I can stir in some chopped nuts, dark chocolate shavings, or fresh fruit after blending, though I'll need to account for any additional points.

Nutritional Information:

- Calories: 110, Protein: 1g, Fat: 0g, Carbohydrates: 28g, Fiber: 4g, Sugar: 19g, Points: 0

Serving Suggestions:

1. Top with Fresh Fruit: I like to garnish the nice cream with a few extra slices of fresh strawberries or bananas for added color and flavor.
2. Serve in a Cone (Optional): For a fun presentation, I can serve the nice cream in a zero-point waffle cone, though I'll need to check the points for the cone.

Poached Pears in Spiced Herbal Tea

Poached Pears in Spiced Herbal Tea is a light, elegant dessert or dinner option that's perfect for satisfying sweet cravings while keeping me on track with my weight loss goals. The pears are gently poached in a fragrant spiced herbal tea, which infuses them with warm, aromatic flavors. This dish is simple to prepare and is a wonderful way to enjoy fruit in a refined, zero-point way.

Prep time: 5 minutes | Cooking time: 20 minutes | Servings: 2

Ingredients (0 points):

- 2 ripe but firm pears, peeled and cored
- 2 cups water
- 2 herbal tea bags (such as cinnamon, chai, or rooibos)
- 1 cinnamon stick
- 2 whole cloves
- 1 teaspoon vanilla extract
- Fresh mint leaves for garnish (optional)

Step-by-Step Directions:

1. Prepare the Poaching Liquid: I begin by bringing 2 cups of water to a gentle simmer in a medium saucepan. Once the water is simmering, I add the herbal tea bags, cinnamon stick, cloves, and vanilla extract. I let the tea steep for about 5 minutes to allow the spices to infuse the water with their flavors.
2. Poach the Pears: While the tea is steeping, I peel and core the pears, leaving them whole. After the tea has steeped, I remove the tea bags and carefully place the pears in the poaching liquid. I allow the pears to poach over low heat for about 15-20 minutes, turning them occasionally to ensure they cook evenly. The pears are done when they are tender but still hold their shape. I can test them by piercing them gently with a fork.
3. Cool and Serve: Once the pears are poached to perfection, I remove them from the liquid and set them aside to cool slightly. I can also reduce the poaching liquid by simmering it for a few more minutes to create a slightly thicker sauce, which can be drizzled over the pears. I place each pear on a plate and drizzle with a bit of the spiced poaching liquid. For an elegant touch, I garnish each pear with fresh mint leaves.

Tips:

1. Choose the Right Pears: I select pears that are ripe but still firm to the touch, such as Bosc or Anjou. This ensures they hold their shape during poaching.
2. Experiment with Spices: I can customize the flavor by adding other spices like star anise, cardamom pods, or a strip of orange zest to the poaching liquid.
3. Serve Warm or Cold: These poached pears can be served warm, at room temperature, or chilled, depending on my preference.

Nutritional Information:

- Calories: 80, Protein: 0g, Fat: 0g, Carbohydrates: 21g, Fiber: 4g, Sugar: 14g, Points: 0

Serving Suggestions:

1. Pair with Greek Yogurt (Optional): For a creamy contrast, I can serve these pears with a dollop of fat-free Greek yogurt, though I'll need to check the points for any additions.
2. Serve with a Biscotti (Optional): For a touch of crunch, I can serve the poached pears with a small biscotti or a crispbread, but I'll need to account for the points.

Mixed Berry Sorbet

This Mixed Berry Sorbet is a refreshing and guilt-free dessert that's perfect for satisfying sweet cravings while keeping me on track with my weight loss goals. Made with frozen berries and a splash of lemon juice, this sorbet is naturally sweet, tangy, and full of vibrant flavor. It's a simple and quick recipe that fits perfectly into the Zero Point Weight Loss program.

Prep time: 5 minutes | Cooking time: None | Servings: 2

Ingredients (0 points):

- 2 cups frozen mixed berries (e.g., strawberries, blueberries, raspberries, blackberries)
- 1 tablespoon fresh lemon juice
- A few drops of water (if needed)

Step-by-Step Directions:

1. Prepare the Berries: I start by ensuring my frozen mixed berries are ready to use. I can use a combination of strawberries, blueberries, raspberries, and blackberries, or any other berry mix I prefer.
2. Blend the Sorbet: In a high-powered blender or food processor, I combine the frozen mixed berries and fresh lemon juice. I blend the mixture on high until it reaches a smooth, sorbet-like consistency. If the mixture is too thick to blend, I can add a few drops of water, just enough to help the berries blend smoothly. I stop the blender occasionally to scrape down the sides, ensuring everything is evenly blended.
3. Serve Immediately: Once the sorbet is smooth and creamy, I divide it between two bowls and serve it immediately. The sorbet is best enjoyed fresh, as it will have the perfect texture straight from the blender.

Tips:

1. Adjust Sweetness: If the berries are too tart, I can add a few drops of a zero-calorie sweetener, but this is usually unnecessary as the natural sweetness of the berries should be enough.
2. Add Fresh Herbs: For an extra burst of flavor, I can blend in a few fresh mint leaves or basil with the berries.
3. Make Ahead: If I want to prepare the sorbet ahead of time, I can blend it and then freeze it in an airtight container. I'll just need to let it sit at room temperature for a few minutes before serving to soften.

Nutritional Information:

- Calories: 50, Protein: 1g, Fat: 0g, Carbohydrates: 13g, Fiber: 5g, Sugar: 7g, Points: 0

Serving Suggestions:

1. Pair with Fresh Fruit: I like to serve this sorbet with a few fresh berries on top for added texture and flavor.
2. Serve with a Wedge of Lemon (Optional): For a beautiful presentation, I can garnish the sorbet with a wedge of lemon or a sprig of mint.

Baked Rhubarb with Fresh Strawberries and Vanilla Extract

This Baked Rhubarb with Fresh Strawberries and Vanilla Extract is a delightful and tangy dessert that fits perfectly into the Zero Point Weight Loss program. The natural tartness of the rhubarb is balanced by the sweetness of fresh strawberries, while the vanilla extract adds a warm, aromatic touch. This simple yet flavorful dish is a great way to enjoy a healthy, zero-point treat that's both satisfying and refreshing.

Prep time: 10 minutes | Cooking time: 25 minutes | Servings: 2

Ingredients (0 points):

- 2 cups rhubarb, chopped into 1-inch pieces
- 1 cup fresh strawberries, hulled and halved
- 1 teaspoon vanilla extract
- 1 tablespoon fresh lemon juice
- A few drops of zero-calorie sweetener (optional)

Step-by-Step Directions:

1. Preheat the Oven: I start by preheating my oven to 375°F (190°C). While the oven is heating, I prepare the rhubarb and strawberries.
2. Prepare the Rhubarb and Strawberries: I wash and chop the rhubarb into 1-inch pieces, then hull and halve the strawberries. I place the rhubarb and strawberries in a mixing bowl.
3. Add Flavorings: I add the vanilla extract and fresh lemon juice to the bowl with the rhubarb and strawberries. If I want to balance the tartness, I can add a few drops of zero-calorie sweetener, but this is optional. I toss everything together to ensure the fruit is evenly coated with the flavorings.
4. Bake the Fruit: I transfer the mixture to a baking dish and spread it out in an even layer. I then bake the fruit in the preheated oven for about 25 minutes, or until the rhubarb is tender and the strawberries have released their juices. I check the dish halfway through baking and give it a gentle stir to ensure even cooking.
5. Cool and Serve: Once the fruit is baked to perfection, I remove the dish from the oven and let it cool slightly. I divide the baked rhubarb and strawberries between two bowls and serve them warm or at room temperature.

Tips:

1. Enhance the Flavor: For added depth, I can sprinkle a pinch of ground cinnamon or nutmeg over the fruit before baking.
2. Make It Creamy (Optional): For a creamy contrast, I can serve the baked fruit with a dollop of fat-free Greek yogurt or a drizzle of unsweetened almond milk, though I'll need to check the points for any additions.
3. Store Leftovers: If I have leftovers, I can store them in an airtight container in the refrigerator for up to three days. The flavors will continue to meld, making it even tastier the next day.

Nutritional Information:

- Calories: 60, Protein: 1g, Fat: 0g, Carbohydrates: 15g, Fiber: 4g, Sugar: 9g, Points: 0

Serving Suggestions:

1. Top with Fresh Mint: I like to garnish this dish with a few fresh mint leaves for a pop of color and extra freshness.
2. Serve with a Light Biscuit (Optional): For a more substantial dessert, I can pair the baked fruit with a small, zero-point biscuit or crispbread, though I'll need to account for any additional points.

Citrus Salad with Oranges, Grapefruit, and Mint

This Citrus Salad with Oranges, Grapefruit, and Mint is a refreshing and vibrant dish that's perfect for a light dinner or as a side dish. The bright and juicy citrus fruits are complemented by the fresh mint, creating a flavorful and hydrating meal that's ideal for the Zero Point Weight Loss program. This salad is easy to prepare, visually appealing, and full of vitamins and antioxidants, making it a healthy choice that doesn't sacrifice taste.

Prep time: 10 minutes | Cooking time: None | Servings: 2

Ingredients (0 points):

- 2 large oranges, peeled and sliced into rounds
- 1 large grapefruit, peeled and sliced into rounds
- 1 tablespoon fresh mint leaves, chopped
- 1 teaspoon fresh lime juice

Step-by-Step Directions:

1. Prepare the Citrus Fruits: I start by peeling the oranges and grapefruit, making sure to remove as much of the white pith as possible. I then slice the fruits into rounds, about 1/4-inch thick. Assemble the Salad: I arrange the orange and grapefruit slices on a large plate or platter, alternating between the two fruits to create a beautiful pattern. I drizzle the fresh lime juice over the citrus slices, which adds a touch of acidity and enhances the natural flavors of the fruit.
2. Add the Mint: I sprinkle the chopped fresh mint leaves over the top of the citrus salad. The mint adds a refreshing and aromatic element that pairs perfectly with the citrus fruits.
3. Serve: I divide the salad between two plates, serving it immediately while the fruits are fresh and juicy. This salad is best enjoyed right after it's prepared, as the mint and lime juice will be at their most vibrant.

Tips:

1. Add Extra Flavor: For a bit more depth, I can add a pinch of ground cinnamon or a few thinly sliced red onions to the salad.
2. Chill Before Serving: If I prefer my salad cold, I can refrigerate the citrus slices for about 20 minutes before assembling the salad.
3. Use a Mix of Citrus Fruits: For variety, I can include other citrus fruits like blood oranges or tangerines in the salad.

Nutritional Information:

- Calories: 90, Protein: 2g, Fat: 0g, Carbohydrates: 23g, Fiber: 5g, Sugar: 18g, Points: 0

Serving Suggestions:

1. Pair with a Light Protein: I like to serve this salad with a light protein like grilled chicken breast or shrimp for a more substantial meal.
2. Serve as a Side Dish: This citrus salad also works well as a side dish alongside other zero-point meals, adding a burst of color and freshness to the plate.

Grilled Pineapple Rings with a Dusting of Cinnamon

Grilled Pineapple Rings with a Dusting of Cinnamon is a sweet, satisfying, and incredibly simple dessert or light dinner option that fits perfectly into the Zero Point Weight Loss program. Grilling the pineapple caramelizes its natural sugars, bringing out a deep, rich flavor that's beautifully complemented by a light sprinkle of cinnamon. This dish is quick to prepare, bursting with flavor, and a delightful way to enjoy a healthy, zero-point treat.

Prep time: 5 minutes | Cooking time: 6-8 minutes | Servings: 2

Ingredients (0 points):

- 4 fresh pineapple rings, about 1/2-inch thick
- 1/2 teaspoon ground cinnamon

Step-by-Step Directions:

- Prepare the Pineapple: I start by cutting a fresh pineapple into rings, about 1/2-inch thick. If I'm using a whole pineapple, I'll need to peel, core, and slice it into rings. I can also use pre-sliced pineapple rings for convenience.
- Preheat the Grill: I preheat my grill or grill pan to medium-high heat. While the grill is heating up, I lightly sprinkle each pineapple ring with ground cinnamon on both sides.
- Grill the Pineapple: Once the grill is hot, I place the pineapple rings directly on the grill. I cook them for about 3-4 minutes on each side, or until grill marks appear and the pineapple is heated through. The heat will caramelize the natural sugars in the pineapple, enhancing its sweetness and flavor.
- Serve Immediately: I remove the grilled pineapple rings from the grill and place them on two plates. The rings can be served hot off the grill for the best flavor and texture.

Tips:

1. Add Extra Flavor: For a different twist, I can add a squeeze of fresh lime juice over the pineapple before grilling or sprinkle a pinch of ground ginger for a bit of spice.
2. Make It Savory (Optional): If I prefer a savory-sweet combination, I can pair the grilled pineapple with a sprinkle of sea salt or a drizzle of balsamic glaze (though I'll need to check the points for the glaze).
3. Use a Grill Pan: If I don't have an outdoor grill, a stovetop grill pan works perfectly for this recipe.

Nutritional Information:

- Calories: 50, Protein: 0g, Fat: 0g, Carbohydrates: 13g, Fiber: 1g, Sugar: 10g, Points: 0

Serving Suggestions:

1. Pair with Yogurt (Optional): For a creamy contrast, I like to serve the grilled pineapple with a dollop of fat-free Greek yogurt or a scoop of vanilla-flavored fat-free yogurt (check points if using flavored yogurt).
2. Serve with Fresh Mint: I can garnish the grilled pineapple rings with fresh mint leaves for a pop of color and added freshness.

SNACKS AND APPETIZERS
Deviled Eggs with Greek Yogurt and Mustard Filling

Deviled Eggs with Greek Yogurt and Mustard Filling is a classic snack or appetizer that has been given a healthy twist to fit perfectly into the Zero Point Weight Loss program. By replacing mayonnaise with fat-free Greek yogurt, I get the same creamy texture but with added protein and fewer calories. The tangy mustard adds flavor without adding any points, making this dish both delicious and guilt-free.

Prep time: 10 minutes | Cooking time: 10 minutes (for boiling eggs)| Servings: 2

Ingredients (0 points):

- 4 large eggs
- 1/4 cup fat-free Greek yogurt
- 1 teaspoon Dijon mustard
- 1/2 teaspoon apple cider vinegar
- Salt and pepper to taste
- Paprika for garnish (optional)
- Fresh chives or parsley for garnish (optional)

Step-by-Step Directions:

1. Boil the Eggs: I start by placing the eggs in a saucepan and covering them with water. I bring the water to a boil over medium-high heat. Once the water is boiling, I reduce the heat to low and let the eggs simmer for 10 minutes. After 10 minutes, I transfer the eggs to a bowl of ice water to cool for a few minutes before peeling them.
2. Prepare the Filling: Once the eggs are cooled and peeled, I slice them in half lengthwise and gently remove the yolks, placing them in a small mixing bowl. To the yolks, I add the fat-free Greek yogurt, Dijon mustard, and apple cider vinegar. I mash everything together with a fork until the mixture is smooth and creamy. I season the filling with salt and pepper to taste.
3. Fill the Eggs: I spoon or pipe the yolk mixture back into the egg whites, dividing it evenly among the 8 egg halves. If I want to be fancy, I can use a piping bag to create a more decorative look.
4. Garnish and Serve: I sprinkle a little paprika over the filled eggs for color and a mild smoky flavor. For an extra touch, I can also garnish with fresh chives or parsley.

Tips:

1. Make Ahead: I can prepare these deviled eggs ahead of time and store them in the refrigerator for up to 2 days. They make a great grab-and-go snack.
2. Customize the Flavor: For a different flavor profile, I can add a dash of hot sauce or a pinch of curry powder to the yolk mixture.
3. Use Different Mustards: If I prefer, I can use spicy brown mustard or whole grain mustard instead of Dijon.

Nutritional Information:

Calories: 60, Protein: 6g, Fat: 3g, Carbohydrates: 1g, Fiber: 0g, Sugar: 1g, Points: 0

Serving Suggestions:

1. Pair with Fresh Veggies: I like to serve these deviled eggs with a side of fresh vegetable sticks like celery, cucumber, or bell peppers for a crunchy, satisfying snack.
2. Serve as an Appetizer: These deviled eggs make a great appetizer for gatherings, served alongside a simple salad or other zero-point finger foods.

Cucumber Slices with Tuna Salad Topping

Cucumber Slices with Tuna Salad Topping is a light, refreshing, and satisfying snack or appetizer that perfectly fits into the Zero Point Weight Loss program. The cool, crisp cucumber slices provide the perfect base for a protein-packed tuna salad made with celery and Greek yogurt. This dish is quick to prepare, low in calories, and high in protein, making it an ideal choice for a healthy snack that keeps me full without adding points.

Prep time: 10 minutes | Cooking time: None | Servings: 2

Ingredients (0 points):

- 1 large cucumber, sliced into rounds
- 1 can (5 oz) tuna packed in water, drained
- 1/4 cup fat-free Greek yogurt
- 1/4 cup celery, finely chopped
- 1 teaspoon Dijon mustard
- 1/2 teaspoon fresh lemon juice
- Salt and pepper to taste
- Fresh dill or parsley for garnish (optional)

Step-by-Step Directions:

1. Prepare the Tuna Salad: I start by draining the canned tuna and placing it in a medium mixing bowl. I then add the finely chopped celery, fat-free Greek yogurt, Dijon mustard, and fresh lemon juice. I mix everything together until well combined. I season the tuna salad with salt and pepper to taste, adjusting the seasoning as needed.
2. Slice the Cucumber: While preparing the tuna salad, I wash and slice the cucumber into rounds, about 1/4-inch thick. The cucumber slices should be thick enough to hold the tuna salad without breaking.
3. Assemble the Appetizer: I arrange the cucumber slices on a serving plate. Using a spoon, I carefully top each cucumber slice with a generous dollop of the tuna salad, spreading it evenly. If I want to add a touch of color and extra flavor, I can garnish each cucumber-tuna bite with a small sprig of fresh dill or parsley.
4. Serve Immediately: I serve the cucumber slices with tuna salad topping immediately while the cucumbers are fresh and crisp. This appetizer is best enjoyed cold.

Tips:

1. Add Extra Crunch: For added texture, I can mix in some finely chopped red onion or bell pepper into the tuna salad.
2. Make it Spicy: If I prefer a bit of heat, I can add a dash of hot sauce or a pinch of red pepper flakes to the tuna salad mixture.
3. Use Different Bases: If I want to switch things up, I can serve the tuna salad on other zero-point bases like bell pepper rings or endive leaves.

Nutritional Information:

Calories: 90, Protein: 16g, Fat: 1g, Carbohydrates: 3g, Fiber: 1g, Sugar: 2g, Points: 0

Serving Suggestions:

1. Pair with Soup: I like to pair these cucumber tuna bites with a light, zero-point soup like a vegetable broth for a more substantial meal.
2. Serve as a Party Appetizer: These cucumber slices with tuna salad topping make a great party appetizer, as they're easy to eat and visually appealing.

Roasted Red Pepper and Tomato Soup

Roasted Red Pepper and Tomato Soup is a flavorful and comforting snack or appetizer that fits perfectly into the Zero Point Weight Loss program. The rich, smoky flavors of roasted red peppers blend beautifully with sweet, juicy tomatoes to create a warming soup that's both satisfying and nutritious. This recipe is simple to prepare and packed with vitamins and antioxidants, making it a great choice for a light, healthy meal.

Prep time: 10 minutes | Cooking time: 30 minutes | Servings: 2

Ingredients (0 points):

- 2 large red bell peppers, halved and seeded
- 4 large tomatoes, quartered
- 1 small onion, chopped
- 2 cloves garlic, minced
- 2 cups vegetable broth
- 1 teaspoon fresh thyme leaves (or 1/2 teaspoon dried thyme)
- 1/2 teaspoon smoked paprika (optional, for added smokiness)
- Salt and pepper to taste
- Fresh basil or parsley for garnish (optional)

Step-by-Step Directions:

1. Roast the Vegetables: I start by preheating my oven to 425°F (220°C). I then place the halved red bell peppers and quartered tomatoes on a baking sheet, skin side up. I drizzle them lightly with cooking spray or a small amount of water to prevent sticking. I roast the vegetables in the preheated oven for about 20 minutes, or until the skins of the peppers are charred and the tomatoes are soft. I remove the vegetables from the oven and let them cool slightly.
2. Prepare the Soup Base: While the vegetables are roasting, I heat a large pot over medium heat and add the chopped onion and minced garlic. I sauté them until the onion is translucent and the garlic is fragrant, about 5 minutes.
3. Blend the Soup: Once the roasted vegetables are cool enough to handle, I peel the charred skins off the red peppers. I then add the roasted peppers and tomatoes to the pot with the sautéed onions and garlic. I pour in the vegetable broth and add the fresh thyme leaves and smoked paprika (if using). I bring the mixture to a simmer and cook for about 10 minutes to allow the flavors to meld.
4. Puree the Soup: Using an immersion blender, I puree the soup until it's smooth and creamy. If I don't have an immersion blender, I can carefully transfer the soup in batches to a regular blender and blend until smooth, then return it to the pot.
5. Season and Serve: I taste the soup and season it with salt and pepper as needed. I then divide the soup between two bowls and garnish each serving with fresh basil or parsley if desired.

Tips:

1. Add Extra Depth: For a richer flavor, I can add a splash of balsamic vinegar or a squeeze of fresh lemon juice before serving.
2. Make it Spicy: If I prefer a bit of heat, I can add a pinch of red pepper flakes or a dash of hot sauce to the soup.
3. Store Leftovers: This soup can be stored in an airtight container in the refrigerator for up to 3 days or frozen for longer storage.

Nutritional Information:

- Calories: 80, Protein: 3g, Fat: 0g, Carbohydrates: 19g, Fiber: 5g, Sugar: 12g, Points: 0

Serving Suggestions:

1. Pair with a Side Salad: I like to serve this soup with a fresh green salad on the side for a light, balanced meal.

Fresh Veggie Platter with Homemade Salsa or Pico de Gallo

This Fresh Veggie Platter with Homemade Salsa or Pico de Gallo is a colorful, crunchy, and refreshing snack or appetizer that fits perfectly into the Zero Point Weight Loss program. The platter features a variety of fresh, crisp vegetables served alongside a zesty, homemade salsa or pico de gallo. This dish is perfect for sharing, easy to prepare, and packed with vitamins and fiber, making it an ideal choice for a light, healthy snack that keeps me satisfied without adding any points.

Prep time: 15 minutes | Cooking time: None | Servings: 2

Ingredients (0 points):

- For the Veggie Platter:
- 1 large cucumber, sliced into rounds or sticks
- 1 red bell pepper, sliced into strips
- 1 yellow bell pepper, sliced into strips
- 1 cup cherry tomatoes, halved
- 2 medium carrots, peeled and sliced into sticks
- 1 cup sugar snap peas
- 1 cup radishes, halved or sliced

- For the Homemade Salsa or Pico de Gallo:
- 2 large tomatoes, diced
- 1/4 cup red onion, finely chopped
- 1/4 cup fresh cilantro, chopped
- 1 jalapeño pepper, seeded and finely chopped (optional) (0 points)
- 1 tablespoon fresh lime juice
- Salt and pepper to taste

Step-by-Step Directions:

1. Prepare the Veggies: I start by washing and slicing all the vegetables for the platter. I arrange the cucumber slices, bell pepper strips, cherry tomatoes, carrot sticks, sugar snap peas, and radishes on a large serving platter, creating a colorful and appealing display.
2. Make the Salsa or Pico de Gallo: In a medium mixing bowl, I combine the diced tomatoes, finely chopped red onion, fresh cilantro, and jalapeño pepper (if using). I add the fresh lime juice and season with salt and pepper to taste. I gently toss all the ingredients together until well combined. If I prefer a chunkier salsa, I can leave it as is, or I can pulse the mixture in a food processor for a smoother consistency.
3. Serve: I place the bowl of homemade salsa or pico de gallo in the center of the veggie platter. This creates a vibrant, healthy snack that's perfect for dipping and sharing.

Tips:

1. Customize Your Veggies: I can mix and match the vegetables based on what I have on hand or what's in season. Other great options include celery sticks, broccoli florets, or zucchini rounds.
2. Spice it Up: If I enjoy a bit of heat, I can add more jalapeño or even a dash of hot sauce to the salsa for an extra kick.
3. Make Ahead: The salsa or pico de gallo can be made ahead of time and stored in the refrigerator for up to 2 days. This makes it easy to prepare the platter just before serving.

Nutritional Information:

- Calories: 70, Protein: 3g, Fat: 0g, Carbohydrates: 16g, Fiber: 6g, Sugar: 10g, Points: 0

Serving Suggestions:

1. Pair with Grilled Protein: For a more substantial snack, I like to serve this veggie platter alongside grilled chicken strips or shrimp, though I'll need to check the points for any added protein.
2. Serve as a Party Appetizer: This veggie platter with homemade salsa is perfect for parties and gatherings, offering a healthy, zero-point option that everyone can enjoy.

Zucchini Chips with a Sprinkle of Garlic Powder and Paprika

Zucchini Chips with a Sprinkle of Garlic Powder and Paprika are a healthy, crunchy, and flavorful snack that fits perfectly into the Zero Point Weight Loss program. These baked zucchini chips are seasoned with simple spices and offer a satisfying alternative to traditional potato chips, without any of the guilt. This recipe is easy to prepare and provides a delicious way to enjoy a savory snack while staying on track with weight loss goals.

Prep time: 10 minutes | Cooking time: 2 hours | Servings: 2

Ingredients (0 points):

- 1 large zucchini, thinly sliced into rounds
- 1/2 teaspoon garlic powder
- 1/2 teaspoon paprika
- Salt and pepper to taste

Step-by-Step Directions:

1. Preheat the Oven: I start by preheating my oven to 225°F (110°C). This low temperature ensures that the zucchini chips will dry out slowly and become crispy without burning.
2. Prepare the Zucchini: Using a sharp knife or a mandoline slicer, I slice the zucchini into thin, even rounds. The slices should be about 1/8-inch thick to ensure they crisp up properly.
3. Season the Zucchini: I place the zucchini slices in a large bowl and sprinkle them with garlic powder, paprika, salt, and pepper. I toss the slices gently to ensure they are evenly coated with the seasonings.
4. Arrange on a Baking Sheet: I line a baking sheet with parchment paper to prevent sticking, then arrange the zucchini slices in a single layer on the sheet. It's important that the slices don't overlap, as this can cause them to steam instead of crisping up.
5. Bake the Zucchini Chips: I bake the zucchini slices in the preheated oven for about 2 hours, flipping them halfway through the cooking time to ensure even crisping. The chips are ready when they are golden brown and crispy.
6. Cool and Serve: Once the zucchini chips are done baking, I remove them from the oven and let them cool on the baking sheet for a few minutes. This allows them to crisp up even more. I then divide the chips between two servings and enjoy them immediately.

Tips:

1. Use a Mandoline for Even Slices: To ensure the zucchini chips cook evenly, I find it helpful to use a mandoline slicer for consistent thickness.
2. Add Extra Flavor: For a different flavor profile, I can sprinkle the zucchini slices with other spices like cayenne pepper, onion powder, or dried herbs before baking.
3. Store Leftovers: If I have any leftover chips (though they're usually eaten quickly!), I can store them in an airtight container at room temperature for up to 2 days.

Nutritional Information:

- Calories: 40, Protein: 2g, Fat: 0g, Carbohydrates: 8g, Fiber: 2g, Sugar: 3g, Points: 0

Serving Suggestions:

1. Pair with a Dip: These zucchini chips are delicious on their own, but I also enjoy pairing them with a zero-point dip like salsa or a yogurt-based dip for added flavor.
2. Serve as a Side: I can serve these chips alongside a zero-point sandwich or wrap for a crunchy, satisfying side dish.

Spicy Roasted Chickpeas with Cumin and Paprika

Spicy Roasted Chickpeas with Cumin and Paprika is a crunchy, flavorful snack that fits perfectly into the Zero Point Weight Loss program. These roasted chickpeas are seasoned with a blend of spices, offering a satisfying, protein-packed alternative to traditional snacks. This recipe is easy to prepare and makes for a great on-the-go snack or appetizer that keeps me full without adding any points.

Prep time: 5 minutes | Cooking time: 30-35 minutes | Servings: 2

Ingredients (0 points):

- 1 can (15 oz) chickpeas, drained and rinsed
- 1 teaspoon ground cumin
- 1 teaspoon smoked paprika
- 1/2 teaspoon garlic powder
- 1/4 teaspoon cayenne pepper (optional, for extra spice)
- Salt and pepper to taste
- Cooking spray or a few drops of water to coat

Step-by-Step Directions:

1. Preheat the Oven: I start by preheating my oven to 400°F (200°C). While the oven heats, I prepare the chickpeas.
2. Prepare the Chickpeas: After draining and rinsing the chickpeas, I spread them out on a clean kitchen towel or paper towels to dry thoroughly. Drying the chickpeas well helps them crisp up better in the oven.
3. Season the Chickpeas: I place the dried chickpeas in a large mixing bowl and lightly coat them with cooking spray or a few drops of water. This helps the spices adhere to the chickpeas. I add the ground cumin, smoked paprika, garlic powder, cayenne pepper (if using), salt, and pepper to the bowl. I toss the chickpeas until they are evenly coated with the spice mixture.
4. Roast the Chickpeas: I spread the seasoned chickpeas in a single layer on a baking sheet lined with parchment paper. It's important that they are in an even layer to ensure they roast evenly. I roast the chickpeas in the preheated oven for 30-35 minutes, shaking the baking sheet halfway through cooking to ensure even roasting. The chickpeas are ready when they are golden brown and crispy.
5. Cool and Serve: Once the chickpeas are roasted, I remove them from the oven and let them cool slightly. I divide them between two servings and enjoy them while they are still warm and crunchy.

Tips:

1. Adjust the Spice Level: If I prefer a milder flavor, I can reduce or omit the cayenne pepper. Conversely, for extra heat, I can add more cayenne or a pinch of chili powder.
2. Store Leftovers: If I have leftovers, I store them in an airtight container at room temperature. However, chickpeas tend to lose their crispiness over time, so they're best enjoyed fresh.
3. Experiment with Spices: I can customize the flavor by experimenting with different spice blends, such as adding curry powder, smoked paprika, or ground coriander.

Nutritional Information:

- Calories: 120, Protein: 6g, Fat: 2g, Carbohydrates: 20g, Fiber: 6g, Sugar: 1g, Points: 0

Serving Suggestions:

1. Pair with Veggies: I like to pair these spicy roasted chickpeas with fresh vegetable sticks like cucumber, bell peppers, or celery for a more filling snack.
2. Use as a Salad Topper: These chickpeas also make a great crunchy topping for salads, adding both flavor and texture.

Baked Eggplant Slices with Marinara Dipping Sauce

Baked Eggplant Slices with Marinara Dipping Sauce is a healthy and delicious snack or appetizer that fits perfectly into the Zero Point Weight Loss program. These baked eggplant slices are tender on the inside and slightly crispy on the outside, making them a satisfying alternative to fried snacks. Paired with a flavorful marinara dipping sauce, this dish is full of taste and completely guilt-free.

Prep time: 10 minutes | Cooking time: 25 minutes | Servings: 2

Ingredients (0 points):

- 1 large eggplant, sliced into 1/4-inch thick rounds
- 1/2 teaspoon garlic powder
- 1/2 teaspoon onion powder
- 1/2 teaspoon dried oregano
- Salt and pepper to taste
- Cooking spray

- For the Marinara Dipping Sauce:
- 1 cup crushed tomatoes
- 1/2 teaspoon garlic powder
- 1/2 teaspoon onion powder
- 1/2 teaspoon dried basil or oregano
- Salt and pepper to taste

Step-by-Step Directions:

1. Preheat the Oven: I start by preheating my oven to 400°F (200°C). I then line a baking sheet with parchment paper or lightly spray it with cooking spray to prevent sticking.
2. Prepare the Eggplant Slices: I slice the eggplant into 1/4-inch thick rounds, making sure the slices are even for consistent baking. I place the eggplant slices in a single layer on the prepared baking sheet.
3. Season the Eggplant: In a small bowl, I mix together the garlic powder, onion powder, dried oregano, salt, and pepper. I sprinkle this seasoning mixture evenly over both sides of the eggplant slices. I then lightly spray the top of the slices with cooking spray to help them crisp up in the oven.
4. Bake the Eggplant: I bake the eggplant slices in the preheated oven for about 20-25 minutes, flipping them halfway through the cooking time. The eggplant is ready when it's tender and lightly browned on the edges.
5. Prepare the Marinara Dipping Sauce: While the eggplant is baking, I prepare the marinara sauce. In a small saucepan, I combine the crushed tomatoes, garlic powder, onion powder, and dried basil or oregano. I season the sauce with salt and pepper to taste. I bring the sauce to a simmer over medium heat and let it cook for about 10 minutes, stirring occasionally, until it's thickened and flavorful.
6. Serve the Eggplant Slices: Once the eggplant slices are baked to perfection, I remove them from the oven and let them cool slightly. I divide the slices between two plates and serve them with a small bowl of marinara sauce on the side for dipping.

Tips:

1. Add Extra Flavor: If I like, I can sprinkle a bit of grated Parmesan cheese on the eggplant slices before baking, though I'll need to account for the points if using cheese.
2. Make it Crispy: For an even crispier texture, I can place the baked eggplant slices under the broiler for the last 1-2 minutes of baking.
3. Use Different Dips: If I want to switch things up, I can serve the eggplant slices with a zero-point yogurt-based dip or even a light salsa.

Nutritional Information:

- Calories: 80, Protein: 2g, Fat: 1g, Carbohydrates: 18g, Fiber: 7g, Sugar: 10g, Points: 0

Serving Suggestions:

1. Serve as an Appetizer: These baked eggplant slices make a great appetizer for a healthy meal, especially when paired with other zero-point snacks like fresh veggie sticks or roasted chickpeas.

Fresh Veggie Spring Rolls with Lettuce, Cucumber, Carrots, and Mint
(No Rice Paper or Noodles)

These Fresh Veggie Spring Rolls are a light, refreshing, and completely zero-point snack that fits perfectly into the Zero Point Weight Loss program. Instead of traditional rice paper or noodles, I use large lettuce leaves as the wrap, which keeps the rolls light and low in points. The combination of crunchy cucumber, crisp carrots, and fresh mint makes these spring rolls a delightful, healthy snack or appetizer that's both satisfying and bursting with flavor.

Prep time: 15 minutes | Cooking time: None | Servings: 2

Ingredients (0 points):

- 6 large lettuce leaves (such as Romaine or Bibb lettuce) (0 points)
- 1 small cucumber, julienned (0 points)
- 1 medium carrot, julienned (0 points)
- 1/4 cup fresh mint leaves
- 1/4 cup fresh cilantro leaves (optional)
- 1/2 red bell pepper, julienned
- 1 tablespoon fresh lime juice

Step-by-Step Directions:

1. Prepare the Vegetables: I start by washing and drying all the vegetables. I then julienne the cucumber, carrot, and red bell pepper into thin strips, which makes them easy to roll up in the lettuce leaves.
2. Assemble the Spring Rolls: I lay out one large lettuce leaf on a flat surface. I place a few strips of cucumber, carrot, and red bell pepper in the center of the leaf. I then add a few mint leaves and cilantro leaves (if using) on top of the vegetables. I drizzle a small amount of fresh lime juice over the vegetables to add a bright, tangy flavor.
3. Roll the Lettuce:I carefully roll up the lettuce leaf, tucking in the sides as I go to create a tight wrap around the vegetables. I repeat this process with the remaining lettuce leaves and vegetables until I have six spring rolls.
4. Serve Immediately: Once the spring rolls are assembled, I cut each roll in half (if desired) and serve them immediately. These rolls are best enjoyed fresh while the vegetables are crisp.

Tips:

1. Add Extra Crunch: For a different texture, I can add a few strips of jicama or radish to the rolls.
2. Use Different Herbs: If I prefer, I can substitute basil or parsley for the mint and cilantro to change the flavor profile.
3. Make a Dipping Sauce: While these spring rolls are delicious on their own, I can pair them with a zero-point dipping sauce like a soy-ginger sauce or a vinegar-based dip.

Nutritional Information:

- Calories: 35, Protein: 1g, Fat: 0g, Carbohydrates: 8g, Fiber: 2g, Sugar: 3g, Points: 0

Serving Suggestions:

1. Pair with Soup: I like to serve these fresh veggie spring rolls alongside a light, zero-point soup like miso or vegetable broth for a more filling snack.
2. Serve as an Appetizer: These rolls make a great appetizer for a healthy meal, especially when paired with other zero-point snacks like zucchini chips or spicy roasted chickpeas.

Grilled Asparagus Spears with Lemon Zest and Sea Salt

Grilled Asparagus Spears with Lemon Zest and Sea Salt is a simple, delicious, and zero-point snack or appetizer that fits perfectly into the Zero Point Weight Loss program. The asparagus spears are lightly grilled to bring out their natural sweetness, and the addition of fresh lemon zest and a sprinkle of sea salt elevates the flavor without adding any extra points. This dish is quick to prepare and makes for a healthy, satisfying snack that's full of nutrients.

Prep time: 5 minutes | Cooking time: 8-10 minutes | Servings: 2

Ingredients (0 points):

- 1 bunch of asparagus (about 12-15 spears), trimmed
- Zest of 1 lemon
- 1/2 teaspoon sea salt
- Cooking spray

Step-by-Step Directions:

1. Preheat the Grill: I start by preheating my grill or grill pan to medium-high heat. While the grill is heating up, I prepare the asparagus.
2. Prepare the Asparagus: I rinse the asparagus spears under cold water and trim the tough ends. I then pat them dry with a paper towel. I place the asparagus in a bowl and lightly spray them with cooking spray, tossing to coat evenly.
3. Grill the Asparagus: I place the asparagus spears on the hot grill in a single layer. I grill them for about 4-5 minutes on each side, turning occasionally, until they are tender and have nice grill marks. The grilling time may vary depending on the thickness of the spears.
4. Add Lemon Zest and Sea Salt: Once the asparagus is grilled to perfection, I remove the spears from the grill and transfer them to a serving plate. I immediately sprinkle the grilled asparagus with the freshly grated lemon zest and a pinch of sea salt. The lemon zest adds a bright, citrusy flavor that pairs perfectly with the natural taste of the asparagus.
5. Serve Immediately: I divide the asparagus spears between two servings and enjoy them right away while they are still warm and full of flavor.

Tips:

1. Use Fresh Asparagus: For the best flavor and texture, I always use fresh, firm asparagus. If the spears are thicker, I may want to peel the lower part of the stems for a more tender result.
2. Add Extra Flavor: If I want to add a little more depth of flavor, I can drizzle a few drops of balsamic vinegar or a squeeze of fresh lemon juice over the asparagus before serving.
3. Cook on a Stovetop: If I don't have access to an outdoor grill, a stovetop grill pan or even a regular skillet works just as well.

Nutritional Information:

- Calories: 20, Protein: 2g, Fat: 0g, Carbohydrates: 4g, Fiber: 2g, Sugar: 2g, Points: 0

Serving Suggestions:

1. Pair with Protein: I like to serve these grilled asparagus spears alongside grilled chicken or fish for a light, zero-point meal.
2. Use as a Side Dish: These asparagus spears make an excellent side dish for any main course, adding a fresh, vibrant touch to the meal.

DRINKS RECIPES
Cucumber and Mint Infused Water

Cucumber and Mint Infused Water is a refreshing and hydrating drink that fits perfectly into the Zero Point Weight Loss program. This drink combines the crisp, cooling flavor of cucumber with the refreshing taste of mint, creating a simple yet flavorful beverage that's not only zero points but also helps me stay hydrated throughout the day. It's a great way to add a little extra enjoyment to plain water without adding any calories or points.

Prep time: 5 minutes | Infusion time: 1 hour (for best flavor)| Servings: 2

Ingredients (0 points):

- 1/2 large cucumber, thinly sliced
- 1/4 cup fresh mint leaves
- 1 liter of cold water
- Ice cubes (optional)

Step-by-Step Directions:

1. Prepare the Ingredients: I start by washing the cucumber and mint leaves thoroughly. I then slice the cucumber into thin rounds, leaving the peel on for added flavor and nutrients. I gently tear the mint leaves to release their natural oils.
2. Combine the Ingredients: I place the cucumber slices and mint leaves into a large pitcher. I then pour the cold water over the cucumber and mint, making sure they are fully submerged. If I want to serve the drink immediately, I can add a few ice cubes to chill the water faster.
3. Infuse the Water: For the best flavor, I let the water sit in the refrigerator for at least 1 hour to allow the cucumber and mint to infuse fully. The longer it sits, the more intense the flavor becomes.
4. Serve the Infused Water: Once the water is infused, I stir it gently and then divide it between two glasses. I garnish each glass with an extra slice of cucumber or a sprig of mint if desired, and serve it cold.

Tips:

1. Experiment with Flavors: If I want to mix things up, I can add other zero-point ingredients like lemon slices, lime slices, or even a few fresh berries to the water for different flavor combinations.
2. Reuse the Ingredients (0 points): After finishing the infused water, I can refill the pitcher with more water and let it infuse again. The flavor may be lighter, but it's still delicious.
3. Stay Hydrated: Keeping a pitcher of cucumber and mint-infused water in the fridge encourages me to drink more water throughout the day, supporting my hydration and weight loss goals.

Nutritional Information:

- Calories: 0, Protein: 0g, Fat: 0g, Carbohydrates: 0g, Fiber: 0g, Sugar: 0g, Points: 0

Serving Suggestions:

1. Pair with Meals: I like to serve this cucumber and mint-infused water alongside meals, especially during warm weather, as it's light, refreshing, and complements a variety of dishes.
2. Bring on the Go: I can easily pour this infused water into a reusable water bottle and take it with me on the go to stay hydrated throughout the day.

Iced Green Tea with Fresh Lemon Slices

Iced Green Tea with Fresh Lemon Slices is a refreshing and antioxidant-rich drink that fits perfectly into the Zero Point Weight Loss program. This simple recipe combines the light, earthy flavor of green tea with the bright, tangy taste of fresh lemon, creating a thirst-quenching beverage that's perfect for any time of day. It's a zero-point drink that not only hydrates but also provides a healthy boost to my metabolism.

Prep time: 5 minutes | Brewing time: 5 minutes | Chilling Time: 30 minutes (optional for colder tea) | Servings: 2

Ingredients (0 points):

- 2 green tea bags
- 4 cups boiling water
- 1 fresh lemon, sliced into rounds
- Ice cubes (optional)

Step-by-Step Directions:

1. Brew the Green Tea: I start by boiling 4 cups of water. Once the water is boiling, I remove it from the heat and add the green tea bags. I let the tea steep for about 5 minutes, allowing it to develop a rich flavor. If I prefer a stronger tea, I can steep it for an additional 1-2 minutes.
2. Chill the Tea (Optional): After steeping, I remove the tea bags and let the tea cool to room temperature. If I want my green tea to be iced, I place it in the refrigerator for about 30 minutes to chill.
3. Add Fresh Lemon Slices: Once the tea is cooled or chilled, I prepare the lemon slices. I wash the lemon thoroughly and slice it into thin rounds. I then add the lemon slices directly to the tea, gently stirring to infuse the lemon flavor.
4. Serve the Iced Green Tea: I fill two glasses with ice cubes if I prefer my tea extra cold, then pour the lemon-infused green tea over the ice. I can also garnish each glass with an additional lemon slice on the rim for a touch of elegance.

Tips:

1. Sweeten if Desired: If I prefer a sweeter taste, I can add a zero-calorie sweetener like stevia, but I need to ensure it's within the zero-point guidelines.
2. Experiment with Flavors: I can easily change up the flavor by adding fresh mint leaves or a splash of lime juice to the tea.
3. Make a Big Batch: I like to brew a large batch of this iced green tea and keep it in the refrigerator, so I always have a refreshing, zero-point drink on hand.

Nutritional Information:

- Calories: 0, Protein: 0g, Fat: 0g, Carbohydrates: 0g, Fiber: 0g, Sugar: 0g, Points: 0

Serving Suggestions:

1. Pair with a Light Snack: This iced green tea pairs well with a light, zero-point snack like fresh fruit or vegetable sticks for a refreshing and healthy combo.
2. Perfect for Hot Days: This drink is especially refreshing on a hot day or after a workout, providing a cool and hydrating boost without any added calories.

Mixed Berry and Spinach Smoothie (Using Water or Unsweetened Almond Milk)

This Mixed Berry and Spinach Smoothie is a nutritious and refreshing drink that fits perfectly into the Zero Point Weight Loss program. Combining the sweet and tangy flavors of mixed berries with the nutrient-rich spinach, this smoothie is both satisfying and healthy. Whether I use water or unsweetened almond milk, this smoothie remains a zero-point option, making it an ideal choice for breakfast, a snack, or even a post-workout drink.

Prep time: 5 minutes | Cooking time: None | Servings: 2

Ingredients (0 points):

- 1 cup mixed berries (fresh or frozen)
- 1 cup fresh spinach leaves
- 1 cup water or unsweetened almond milk
- 1/2 banana (optional, for added creaminess)
- Ice cubes (optional, if using fresh berries)

Step-by-Step Directions:

1. Prepare the Ingredients: I start by washing the fresh berries and spinach leaves thoroughly. If I'm using frozen berries, I can add them directly to the blender.
2. Combine the Ingredients: I place the mixed berries, spinach, and water or unsweetened almond milk into a blender. If I want a creamier texture, I can add half a banana. I also add a few ice cubes if I'm using fresh berries and want a colder smoothie.
3. Blend the Smoothie: I blend the ingredients on high speed until the mixture is smooth and creamy. I may need to stop and scrape down the sides of the blender to ensure everything is well combined.
4. Serve Immediately: Once the smoothie is blended to my desired consistency, I divide it between two glasses and serve it immediately. This smoothie is best enjoyed fresh.

Tips:

1. Boost the Nutrition: If I want to add more nutrition, I can toss in a tablespoon of chia seeds or ground flaxseed, though I'll need to check the points for these additions.
2. Adjust the Sweetness: If I prefer a sweeter smoothie, I can add a few drops of a zero-calorie sweetener like stevia. The natural sweetness from the berries and banana usually makes this unnecessary.
3. Store Leftovers: If I have any leftovers, I can store the smoothie in the refrigerator for up to 24 hours, though it's best consumed fresh.

Nutritional Information:

- Calories: 60, Protein: 1g, Fat: 1g, Carbohydrates: 14g, Fiber: 4g, Sugar: 7g, Points: 0

Serving Suggestions:

1. Pair with Breakfast: This smoothie pairs well with a light breakfast, like scrambled eggs or a slice of whole-grain toast, for a balanced meal.
2. Great Post-Workout: I find this smoothie to be an excellent post-workout drink, providing hydration and replenishing nutrients without any added points.

Spiced Herbal Tea with Cinnamon and Ginger

Spiced Herbal Tea with Cinnamon and Ginger is a warming, aromatic drink that perfectly fits into the Zero Point Weight Loss program. This tea combines the soothing properties of herbal tea with the warm, spicy notes of cinnamon and ginger. It's not only comforting but also has metabolism-boosting benefits, making it an ideal drink to enjoy throughout the day.

Prep time: 5 minutes | Cooking time: 10 minutes | Servings: 2

Ingredients (0 points):

- 2 cups water
- 1 cinnamon stick (or 1/2 teaspoon ground cinnamon)
- 1-inch piece of fresh ginger, sliced (or 1/2 teaspoon ground ginger)
- 2 herbal tea bags (such as chamomile, rooibos, or peppermint)
- Lemon slices for garnish (optional)

Step-by-Step Directions:

1. Boil the Water: I start by bringing 2 cups of water to a boil in a small saucepan. Once the water reaches a rolling boil, I reduce the heat to low.
2. Add the Spices: I add the cinnamon stick and sliced ginger to the simmering water. If using ground spices, I simply stir them into the water. I let the spices simmer for about 5-7 minutes, allowing their flavors to infuse into the water.
3. Steep the Herbal Tea: After the spices have infused, I remove the saucepan from the heat and add the herbal tea bags. I cover the saucepan and let the tea steep for about 3-5 minutes, depending on how strong I like it.
4. Strain and Serve: Once the tea has steeped, I remove the tea bags and strain the liquid to remove the cinnamon stick and ginger slices. I pour the tea into two mugs, and if desired, I garnish each mug with a slice of fresh lemon.
5. Enjoy Warm: This spiced herbal tea is best enjoyed warm, making it perfect for a relaxing afternoon or evening.

Tips:

1. Experiment with Herbal Teas: I can try different herbal teas like chamomile, peppermint, or rooibos to vary the flavor profile.
2. Add Sweetness (Optional): If I prefer a slightly sweeter tea, I can add a few drops of a zero-calorie sweetener like stevia, though the natural sweetness from the cinnamon and ginger usually suffices.
3. Make a Large Batch: I can easily double or triple the recipe and store the leftover tea in the refrigerator to reheat later.

Nutritional Information:

- Calories: 0, Protein: 0g, Fat: 0g, Carbohydrates: 0g, Fiber: 0g, Sugar: 0g, Points: 0

Serving Suggestions:

1. Pair with a Light Snack: I like to enjoy this spiced herbal tea with a light, zero-point snack like fresh fruit or a few cucumber slices.
2. Perfect for Relaxation: This tea is particularly soothing in the evening or before bedtime, helping me unwind without adding any points.

Lemon and Lime Sparkling Water with Fresh Mint Leaves

Lemon and Lime Sparkling Water with Fresh Mint Leaves is a refreshing and zesty drink that fits perfectly into the Zero Point Weight Loss program. This drink combines the tangy flavors of lemon and lime with the coolness of fresh mint, all infused into sparkling water. It's a great way to stay hydrated, enjoy a burst of flavor, and add a little sparkle to your day without adding any points.

Prep time: 5 minutes | Cooking time: None | Servings: 2

Ingredients (0 points):

- 2 cups sparkling water
- 1/2 lemon, sliced into rounds
- 1/2 lime, sliced into rounds
- 1/4 cup fresh mint leaves
- Ice cubes (optional)

Step-by-Step Directions:

1. Prepare the Ingredients: I start by washing the lemon, lime, and mint leaves thoroughly. I then slice the lemon and lime into thin rounds, leaving the peels on for added flavor and visual appeal.
2. Combine the Ingredients: I add the lemon and lime slices to a large pitcher or directly into two glasses. I then add the fresh mint leaves, gently muddling them with a spoon to release their natural oils, which enhances the flavor of the drink.
3. Add the Sparkling Water: I pour the sparkling water over the lemon, lime, and mint, allowing the flavors to infuse. If I want my drink extra cold, I can add a few ice cubes at this stage.
4. Serve Immediately: I divide the sparkling water between two glasses, making sure each glass gets an even distribution of the lemon, lime, and mint. I can garnish each glass with an extra slice of lemon or lime and a sprig of mint if desired.

Tips:

1. Adjust the Citrus Flavor: If I prefer a stronger citrus flavor, I can add more lemon or lime slices, or even squeeze a bit of lemon or lime juice into the water before adding the sparkling water.
2. Try Different Herbs: If I want to experiment with flavors, I can substitute the mint with other fresh herbs like basil or rosemary, which also pair well with citrus.
3. Make it in Advance: I can prepare this drink in advance and store it in the refrigerator for a few hours to allow the flavors to meld together even more.

Nutritional Information:

- Calories: 0, Protein: 0g, Fat: 0g, Carbohydrates: 0g, Fiber: 0g, Sugar: 0g, Points: 0

Serving Suggestions:

1. Pair with Meals: This sparkling water pairs well with light meals or snacks, adding a refreshing touch to my dining experience.
2. Great for Gatherings: This drink is perfect for gatherings or parties as a healthy, zero-point alternative to sugary sodas or cocktails.

Watermelon and Basil Infused Water

Watermelon and Basil Infused Water is a light, refreshing, and hydrating drink that fits perfectly into the Zero Point Weight Loss program. The natural sweetness of watermelon paired with the aromatic flavor of fresh basil creates a delightful infusion that's both flavorful and completely zero points. This drink is perfect for staying hydrated while enjoying a burst of summer flavors without adding any extra calories or points.

Prep time: 5 minutes | Cooking time: 1 hour (for best flavor) | Servings: 2

Ingredients (0 points):

- 2 cups of watermelon, cubed
- 1/4 cup fresh basil leaves
- 1 liter of cold water
- Ice cubes (optional)

Step-by-Step Directions:

1. Prepare the Ingredients: I start by cutting the watermelon into small cubes. I also wash the fresh basil leaves thoroughly and gently tear them to release their natural oils, which enhances the flavor of the infused water.
2. Combine the Ingredients: I place the watermelon cubes and basil leaves into a large pitcher. I then pour the cold water over the watermelon and basil, making sure they are fully submerged. If I want to serve the drink immediately, I can add a few ice cubes to chill the water faster.
3. Infuse the Water: For the best flavor, I let the water sit in the refrigerator for at least 1 hour to allow the watermelon and basil to infuse fully. The longer it sits, the more intense the flavor becomes.
4. Serve the Infused Water: Once the water is infused, I stir it gently and then divide it between two glasses. I can garnish each glass with a few extra watermelon cubes or a basil leaf if desired, and serve it cold.

Tips:

1. Experiment with Flavors: If I want to mix things up, I can add other zero-point ingredients like cucumber slices or a splash of lime juice to the water for different flavor combinations.
2. Reuse the Ingredients (0 points): After finishing the infused water, I can refill the pitcher with more water and let it infuse again. The flavor may be lighter, but it's still delicious.
3. Use Fresh Watermelon: For the best taste, I always use fresh, ripe watermelon that's sweet and juicy.

Nutritional Information:

- Calories: 0, Protein: 0g, Fat: 0g, Carbohydrates: 0g, Fiber: 0g, Sugar: 0g, Points: 0

Serving Suggestions:

1. Pair with Meals: This infused water pairs well with light meals, particularly salads or grilled vegetables, adding a refreshing touch to my dining experience.
2. Perfect for Summer: This drink is especially refreshing on a hot day, providing a cool and hydrating option that's bursting with flavor.

Pineapple and Ginger Smoothie (Using Water and Fresh Pineapple Chunks)

This Pineapple and Ginger Smoothie is a refreshing and invigorating drink that fits perfectly into the Zero Point Weight Loss program. The natural sweetness of fresh pineapple combined with the zesty kick of ginger creates a deliciously balanced smoothie that's both satisfying and completely zero points. This smoothie is hydrating, full of vitamins, and perfect for any time of the day.

Prep time: 5 minutes | Cooking time: None | Servings: 2

Ingredients (0 points):

- 1 1/2 cups fresh pineapple chunks
- 1-inch piece of fresh ginger, peeled and sliced
- 1 cup cold water
- Ice cubes (optional)

Step-by-Step Directions:

1. Prepare the Ingredients: I start by peeling and chopping the fresh pineapple into chunks. I also peel and slice the ginger into thin pieces to make blending easier.
2. Combine the Ingredients: I place the pineapple chunks, sliced ginger, and cold water into a blender. If I prefer a colder smoothie, I can add a few ice cubes to the blender.
3. Blend the Smoothie: I blend the ingredients on high speed until the mixture is smooth and creamy. I may need to stop and scrape down the sides of the blender to ensure everything is well combined.
4. Serve Immediately: Once the smoothie is blended to my desired consistency, I divide it between two glasses and serve it immediately. This smoothie is best enjoyed fresh for the most vibrant flavor.

Tips:

1. Adjust the Ginger: If I prefer a milder ginger flavor, I can reduce the amount of ginger used, or if I enjoy a stronger kick, I can add a bit more.
2. Sweeten Naturally (Optional): The natural sweetness of pineapple is usually sufficient, but if I want it sweeter, I can add a few drops of a zero-calorie sweetener like stevia.
3. Store Leftovers: If I have any leftovers, I can store the smoothie in the refrigerator for up to 24 hours, though it's best consumed fresh.

Nutritional Information:

- Calories: 50, Protein: 1g, Fat: 0g, Carbohydrates: 13g, Fiber: 2g, Sugar: 10g, Points: 0

Serving Suggestions:

1. Pair with Breakfast: This smoothie pairs well with a light breakfast, like a hard-boiled egg or a small serving of cottage cheese, for a balanced meal.
2. Post-Workout Refreshment: I find this smoothie to be an excellent post-workout drink, providing hydration and replenishment without any added points.

Celery and Cucumber Juice with a Splash of Lemon

Celery and Cucumber Juice with a Splash of Lemon is a hydrating and refreshing drink that perfectly fits into the Zero Point Weight Loss program. This juice combines the crisp, clean flavors of celery and cucumber with a tangy splash of lemon, creating a light and revitalizing beverage that's full of nutrients and completely zero points. It's an excellent choice for a morning boost or a midday refreshment.

Prep time: 5 minutes | Cooking time: None | Servings: 2

Ingredients (0 points):

- 4 stalks of celery, chopped
- 1 large cucumber, peeled and chopped
- Juice of 1/2 lemon
- 1/2 cup cold water
- Ice cubes (optional)

Step-by-Step Directions:

1. Prepare the Ingredients: I start by washing the celery stalks and cucumber thoroughly. I then chop the celery into smaller pieces and peel and chop the cucumber.
2. Juice the Vegetables: I place the chopped celery and cucumber into a juicer. If I don't have a juicer, I can blend the ingredients in a blender with the cold water until smooth, then strain the juice using a fine-mesh sieve or cheesecloth to remove the pulp.
3. Add the Lemon Juice: Once the juice is prepared, I stir in the juice of half a lemon to add a bright, tangy flavor that complements the freshness of the celery and cucumber.
4. Serve Immediately: I divide the juice between two glasses, adding ice cubes if I prefer it chilled. This juice is best enjoyed fresh to retain its vibrant flavor and nutrients.

Tips:

1. Adjust the Lemon: If I like a more pronounced lemon flavor, I can add more lemon juice to taste. The citrus not only enhances the flavor but also adds a refreshing acidity.
2. Add a Touch of Ginger (Optional): For a little extra zing, I can add a small piece of fresh ginger to the juicer or blender.
3. Store Leftovers: If I have any leftover juice, I can store it in an airtight container in the refrigerator for up to 24 hours, though it's best consumed fresh.

Nutritional Information:

- Calories: 15, Protein: 1g, Fat: 0g, Carbohydrates: 4g, Fiber: 1g, Sugar: 2g, Points: 0

Serving Suggestions:

1. Morning Boost: I find this juice to be a great way to start the day, providing hydration and a light, refreshing flavor that wakes me up.
2. Midday Refreshment: This juice is perfect for a midday pick-me-up, helping me stay hydrated and refreshed without adding any points.

Herbal Iced Tea with Fresh Mint and a Hint of Stevia (Optional)

Herbal Iced Tea with Fresh Mint and a Hint of Stevia is a refreshing, light, and hydrating drink that fits perfectly into the Zero Point Weight Loss program. This tea combines the soothing properties of herbal tea with the cool, invigorating flavor of fresh mint. A hint of stevia can be added for a touch of sweetness, making it a zero-point option that's perfect for any time of the day.

Prep time: 5 minutes | Brewing time: 10 minutes | Chilling Time: 30 minutes (optional for colder tea) | Servings: 2

Ingredients (0 points):

- 2 herbal tea bags (such as peppermint, chamomile, or rooibos)
- 4 cups boiling water
- 1/4 cup fresh mint leaves, lightly crushed
- Stevia to taste (optional)
- Ice cubes (optional)

Step-by-Step Directions:

1. Brew the Herbal Tea: I start by boiling 4 cups of water. Once the water is boiling, I remove it from the heat and add the herbal tea bags. I let the tea steep for about 10 minutes to develop a rich flavor.
2. Add Fresh Mint: While the tea is still warm, I add the fresh mint leaves. I lightly crush the mint leaves with my fingers before adding them to the tea, which helps release their natural oils and enhances the flavor.
3. Sweeten with Stevia (Optional): If I prefer a sweeter tea, I can add a few drops of stevia to the brewed tea. I stir well to ensure the sweetness is evenly distributed.
4. Chill the Tea (Optional): After adding the mint and sweetener, I let the tea cool to room temperature. For iced tea, I can place it in the refrigerator for about 30 minutes to chill.
5. Serve the Iced Tea: I fill two glasses with ice cubes if I prefer my tea extra cold, then pour the mint-infused herbal tea over the ice. I can garnish each glass with an additional mint sprig for a fresh touch.

Tips:

1. Experiment with Herbal Teas: I can try different herbal teas to vary the flavor. Peppermint tea offers a cool, refreshing taste, while chamomile provides a more calming, floral note.
2. Adjust the Sweetness: Stevia is optional, and I can adjust the amount to my liking. The natural flavors of the mint and tea are usually sufficient, but a little sweetness can enhance the drink.
3. Make a Big Batch: I can easily double or triple the recipe and store the leftover tea in the refrigerator to enjoy throughout the day.

Nutritional Information:

- Calories: 0, Protein: 0g, Fat: 0g, Carbohydrates: 0g, Fiber: 0g, Sugar: 0g, Points: 0

Serving Suggestions:

1. Pair with Light Snacks: This herbal iced tea pairs well with light, zero-point snacks like fresh fruit or cucumber slices.
2. Perfect for Warm Days: This drink is especially refreshing on a warm day or after a workout, providing a cool and hydrating boost without any added calories or points.

Tomato and Basil Juice

Tomato and Basil Juice is a refreshing and savory drink that perfectly fits into the Zero Point Weight Loss program. This juice combines the rich, slightly tangy flavor of fresh tomatoes with the aromatic sweetness of basil, creating a delicious beverage that's both hydrating and satisfying. A touch of salt enhances the natural flavors, making it an ideal drink for a light snack or an appetizer.

Prep time: 5 minutes | Cooking time: None | Servings: 2

Ingredients (0 points):

- 4 large ripe tomatoes, chopped
- 1/4 cup fresh basil leaves
- A pinch of salt (optional)
- Ice cubes (optional)

Step-by-Step Directions:

1. Prepare the Ingredients: I start by washing the tomatoes and basil leaves thoroughly. I then chop the tomatoes into smaller pieces to make blending easier.
2. Blend the Tomatoes and Basil: I place the chopped tomatoes and fresh basil leaves into a blender. I blend the mixture on high speed until it becomes a smooth juice. If I prefer a thinner consistency, I can add a little water or strain the juice through a fine-mesh sieve.
3. Season with Salt (Optional): After blending, I add a pinch of salt to enhance the natural flavors. I stir the juice to ensure the salt is evenly distributed.
4. Serve the Juice: I divide the tomato and basil juice between two glasses. If I prefer my juice cold, I can add a few ice cubes to each glass before serving.

Tips:

1. Adjust the Basil: If I prefer a stronger basil flavor, I can add more basil leaves to the juice. The fresh basil adds a delightful aroma and enhances the taste of the tomatoes.
2. Experiment with Additions: For an extra kick, I can add a splash of lemon juice or a pinch of black pepper. These additions can give the juice a more complex flavor profile.
3. Use Fresh, Ripe Tomatoes: For the best taste, I always use ripe, juicy tomatoes, as they provide a naturally sweet and tangy flavor.

Nutritional Information:

- Calories: 20, Protein: 1g, Fat: 0g, Carbohydrates: 5g, Fiber: 1g, Sugar: 3g, Points: 0

Serving Suggestions:

1. Enjoy as a Light Snack: This tomato and basil juice is perfect as a light, refreshing snack between meals.
2. Pair with a Salad: I find this juice pairs well with a simple green salad or a light vegetable dish, making for a healthy and satisfying meal.

Apple and Cinnamon Water

Apple and Cinnamon Water is a simple yet flavorful drink that fits seamlessly into the Zero Point Weight Loss program. This infused water combines the subtle sweetness of fresh apple slices with the warm, aromatic flavor of cinnamon sticks, creating a refreshing and satisfying beverage. It's an easy way to stay hydrated and enjoy a touch of natural flavor without adding any points.

Prep time: 5 minutes | Infusion time: 1 hour (for best flavor)| Servings: 2

Ingredients (0 points):

- 1 apple, thinly sliced
- 2 cinnamon sticks
- 1 liter of cold water
- Ice cubes (optional)

Step-by-Step Directions:

1. Prepare the Ingredients: I begin by washing the apple thoroughly and slicing it thinly, leaving the skin on for added flavor and nutrients. I also gather the cinnamon sticks.
2. Combine the Ingredients: I place the apple slices and cinnamon sticks into a large pitcher. I then pour the cold water over the apples and cinnamon, ensuring they are fully submerged. For a colder drink, I can add a few ice cubes at this stage.
3. Infuse the Water: To allow the flavors to fully develop, I let the water sit in the refrigerator for at least 1 hour. The longer it infuses, the more pronounced the apple and cinnamon flavors will be.
4. Serve the Infused Water: After the infusion period, I stir the water gently and divide it between two glasses. I can garnish each glass with an additional apple slice or a cinnamon stick if desired.

Tips:

1. Experiment with Flavors: If I want to add more depth to the flavor, I can try adding a splash of lemon juice or a few cloves to the infusion.
2. Reuse the Ingredients (0 points): After finishing the water, I can refill the pitcher with more water and let it infuse again. The second infusion may have a lighter flavor but is still enjoyable.
3. Use Fresh Apples: For the best taste, I always use fresh, crisp apples. Varieties like Honeycrisp or Fuji work well due to their natural sweetness.

Nutritional Information:

- Calories: 0, Protein: 0g, Fat: 0g, Carbohydrates: 0g, Fiber: 0g, Sugar: 0g, Points: 0

Serving Suggestions:

1. Enjoy Throughout the Day: This apple and cinnamon water is perfect to sip on throughout the day, helping me stay hydrated with a pleasant flavor.
2. Pair with Light Snacks: I find this drink pairs well with light, zero-point snacks like carrot sticks or a small salad, making for a refreshing and healthy combination.

Kale and Green Apple Smoothie

This Kale and Green Apple Smoothie is a nutritious and refreshing drink that fits perfectly into the Zero Point Weight Loss program. The smoothie combines the slightly tart flavor of green apples with the nutrient-packed goodness of kale. Blended with water or unsweetened almond milk, it creates a satisfying, zero-point beverage that's perfect for a quick breakfast or a midday boost.

Prep time: 5 minutes | Cooking time: None | Servings: 2

Ingredients (0 points):

- 2 cups kale leaves, tough stems removed
- 1 large green apple, cored and chopped
- 1 cup water or unsweetened almond milk
- Ice cubes (optional)

Step-by-Step Directions:

1. Prepare the Ingredients: I start by washing the kale leaves thoroughly and removing the tough stems. I then core and chop the green apple into smaller pieces to make blending easier.
2. Combine the Ingredients: I place the kale leaves, chopped green apple, and water or unsweetened almond milk into a blender. If I want a colder, thicker smoothie, I can add a few ice cubes.
3. Blend the Smoothie: I blend the ingredients on high speed until the mixture is smooth and creamy. Depending on my blender, I may need to stop and scrape down the sides to ensure everything is well combined.
4. Serve Immediately: Once the smoothie is blended to my desired consistency, I divide it between two glasses and serve it immediately. This smoothie is best enjoyed fresh for the most vibrant flavor and nutritional benefit.

Tips:

1. Adjust the Consistency: If the smoothie is too thick for my liking, I can add a bit more water or almond milk to thin it out. Conversely, adding more ice will make it thicker.
2. Add a Hint of Sweetness (Optional): If I prefer a slightly sweeter smoothie, I can add a few drops of a zero-calorie sweetener like stevia, though the natural sweetness of the apple is often enough.
3. Store Leftovers: If I have any leftovers, I can store the smoothie in the refrigerator for up to 24 hours, though it's best consumed fresh.

Nutritional Information:

- Calories: 35, Protein: 1g, Fat: 0g, Carbohydrates: 9g, Fiber: 3g, Sugar: 5g, Points: 0

Serving Suggestions:

1. Perfect for Breakfast: This smoothie makes an excellent start to the day, providing a boost of nutrients and energy without adding any points.
2. Post-Workout Fuel: I find this smoothie to be a great post-workout drink, replenishing my body with hydration and essential vitamins and minerals.

ZERO POINT FOOD LISTS

Here's a general list of zero-point foods that are typically considered part of the Zero Point Weight Loss program, especially in Weight Watchers. These foods are low in calories, high in nutrients, and are meant to be consumed freely without tracking points.

Fruits

Apples	Peaches	Watermelon
Bananas	Pears	Cherries
Blackberries	Pineapples	Cantaloupe
Blueberries	Plums	Kiwi
Grapes	Raspberries	
Oranges	Strawberries	

Vegetables

Artichokes	Cauliflower	Onions
Asparagus	Celery	Peas
Beets	Cucumber	Pumpkin
Bell peppers	Eggplant	Radishes
Broccoli	Green beans	Spinach
Brussels sprouts	Kale	Squash (butternut, acorn, etc.)
Cabbage	Lettuce	Tomatoes
Carrots	Mushrooms	Zucchini

Proteins

Eggs (whole, egg whites)	Shellfish (e.g., shrimp, crab, lobster)	Beans (e.g., black beans, kidney beans, lentils)
Chicken breast (skinless)	Tofu	Chickpeas
Turkey breast (skinless)	Plain, nonfat Greek yogurt	Edamame
Fish (e.g., salmon, tilapia, tuna)		

Non-Starchy Vegetables

Arugula	Swiss chard	Endiv
Bok choy	Turnip greens	
Collard greens	Watercress	

Legumes and Pulses

Black beans

Kidney beans

Lentils

Navy beans

Pinto beans

Split peas

Other Zero-Point Foods

Fat-free salsa

Fat-free broth (vegetable, chicken, or beef)

Pickles (unsweetened)

Sauerkraut (without added sugar)

Vinegar (balsamic, apple cider, etc.)

Mustard

Soy sauce (low sodium)

Herbs and spices

Garlic

Ginger

Beverages

Black coffee

Unsweetened tea

Sparkling water (unsweetened)

Herbal tea (unsweetened)

This list can vary slightly based on different versions of the Weight Watchers program and individual dietary needs. These foods are meant to be the foundation of a healthy diet, providing a range of nutrients while keeping you full and satisfied without the need to track points.

Always check for the latest guidelines if you're following a specific plan, as updates and individual variations can occur.

30-DAY MEAL PLAN

Each day includes breakfast, lunch, dinner, a dessert, a snack, and a drink. This plan ensures variety and balance while adhering to the Zero Point Weight Loss program.

Week 1

Day 1:

Breakfast: Veggie-Packed Scrambled Eggs with Spinach, Mushrooms, and Tomatoes

Lunch: Grilled Chicken Salad with Mixed Greens, Cucumber, Cherry Tomatoes, and Balsamic Vinegar

Dinner: Baked Lemon Herb Chicken with Roasted Brussels Sprouts and Carrots

Dessert: Baked Cinnamon Apples with a Sprinkle of Nutmeg and Fresh Berries

Snack: Deviled Eggs with Greek Yogurt and Mustard Filling

Drink: Cucumber and Mint Infused Water

Day 2:

Breakfast: Greek Yogurt with Mixed Berries and a Sprinkle of Cinnamon

Lunch: Spaghetti Squash with Marinara Sauce and Sautéed Vegetables (Zucchini, Mushrooms, and Spinach)

Dinner: Shrimp and Vegetable Stir-Fry with Bell Peppers, Snow Peas, and Ginger

Dessert: Fresh Fruit Salad with Pineapple, Mango, and Kiwi

Snack: Cucumber Slices with Tuna Salad Topping (made with tuna, celery, and Greek yogurt)

Drink: Iced Green Tea with Fresh Lemon Slices

Day 3:

Breakfast: Egg White Omelet with Bell Peppers, Onions, and Fresh Herbs

Lunch: Tuna Salad Lettuce Wraps with Diced Celery, Red Onion, and Fresh Herbs

Dinner: Grilled Salmon with a Side of Asparagus and Cherry Tomatoes

Dessert: Chilled Mixed Berry Compote with a Dollop of Fat-Free Greek Yogurt

Snack: Roasted Red Pepper and Tomato Soup

Drink: Mixed Berry and Spinach Smoothie (using water or unsweetened almond milk)

Day 4:

Breakfast: Spiced Apple and Oatmeal Breakfast Bowl (using unsweetened applesauce and spices)

Lunch: Grilled Shrimp Skewers with a Side of Roasted Asparagus and Bell Peppers

Dinner: Turkey Meatballs in a Homemade Marinara Sauce with Spaghetti Squash

Dessert: Grilled Peaches with a Drizzle of Balsamic Glaze

Snack: Fresh Veggie Platter with Homemade Salsa or Pico de Gallo

Drink: Spiced Herbal Tea with Cinnamon and Ginger

Day 5:

Breakfast: Cottage Cheese with Sliced Cucumbers and Cherry Tomatoes

Lunch: Turkey and Cabbage Stir-Fry with Ginger and Garlic

Dinner: Grilled Portobello Mushrooms Stuffed with Spinach and Tomatoes

Dessert: Frozen Banana and Strawberry "Nice Cream" (blended frozen bananas and strawberries)

Snack: Zucchini Chips with a Sprinkle of Garlic Powder and Paprika

Drink: Lemon and Lime Sparkling Water with Fresh Mint Leaves

Day 6:

Breakfast: Baked Egg Cups with Zucchini, Red Bell Peppers, and Onions

Lunch: Roasted Vegetable Soup with Butternut Squash, Carrots, and Leeks

Dinner: Pan-Seared Tilapia with a Cucumber and Tomato Salad

Dessert: Poached Pears in Spiced Herbal Tea

Snack: Spicy Roasted Chickpeas with Cumin and Paprika

Drink: Watermelon and Basil Infused Water

Day 7:

Breakfast: Scrambled Tofu with Spinach, Bell Peppers, and Onions

Lunch: Baked Cod with a Side of Steamed Broccoli and Lemon-Garlic Sauce

Dinner: Baked Chicken Breast with Cauliflower Mash and Steamed Green Beans

Dessert: Mixed Berry Sorbet (made with frozen berries and a splash of lemon juice)

Snack: Hard-Boiled Eggs with a Sprinkle of Everything Bagel Seasoning

Drink: Pineapple and Ginger Smoothie (using water and fresh pineapple chunks)

Week 2
Day 8:

Breakfast: Berry Smoothie with Unsweetened Almond Milk and a Handful of Spinach

Lunch: Chickpea and Veggie Salad with Cucumber, Cherry Tomatoes, Red Onion, and Fresh Parsley

Dinner: Stuffed Bell Peppers with Ground Turkey and Diced Vegetables

Dessert: Baked Rhubarb with Fresh Strawberries and Vanilla Extract

Snack: Baked Eggplant Slices with Marinara Dipping Sauce

Drink: Celery and Cucumber Juice with a Splash of Lemon

Day 9:

Breakfast: Poached Eggs over a Bed of Sautéed Kale and Cherry Tomatoes

Lunch: Grilled Turkey Patties with Sautéed Spinach and Mushrooms

Dinner: Grilled Tuna Steak with a Side of Roasted Zucchini and Squash

Dessert: Citrus Salad with Oranges, Grapefruit, and Mint

Snack: Fresh Veggie Spring Rolls with Lettuce, Cucumber, Carrots, and Mint (no rice paper or noodles)

Drink: Herbal Iced Tea with Fresh Mint and a Hint of Stevia (optional)

Day 10:

Breakfast: Fresh Fruit Salad with Grapefruit, Kiwi, and Berries

Lunch: Zucchini Noodles with Tomato Basil Sauce and Grilled Chicken Strips

Dinner: Turkey and Cabbage Rolls with a Tomato-Based Sauce

Dessert: Grilled Pineapple Rings with a Dusting of Cinnamon

Snack: Grilled Asparagus Spears with Lemon Zest and Sea Salt

Drink: Tomato and Basil Juice (fresh tomatoes blended with basil and a touch of salt)

Day 11:

Breakfast: Cauliflower Rice Breakfast Bowl with Sautéed Vegetables and Fresh Herbs

Lunch: Spicy Black Bean Soup with Diced Tomatoes, Onions, and Cilantro

Dinner: Herb-Roasted Chicken Thighs with a Side of Sautéed Spinach and Garlic

Dessert: Baked Cinnamon Apples with a Sprinkle of Nutmeg and Fresh Berries

Snack: Deviled Eggs with Greek Yogurt and Mustard Filling

Drink: Apple and Cinnamon Water (infuse water with apple slices and cinnamon sticks)

Day 12:

Breakfast: Baked Tomato and Egg Cups with Fresh Basil and Oregano

Lunch: Grilled Eggplant and Red Pepper Stack with Fresh Herbs and a Drizzle of Balsamic Vinegar

Dinner: Slow-Cooked Beef Stew with Carrots, Celery, and Onions

Dessert: Fresh Fruit Salad with Pineapple, Mango, and Kiwi

Snack: Cucumber Slices with Tuna Salad Topping (made with tuna, celery, and Greek yogurt)

Drink: Kale and Green Apple Smoothie (using water or unsweetened almond milk)

Day 13:

Breakfast: Greek Yogurt with Mixed Berries and a Sprinkle of Cinnamon

Lunch: Tuna Salad Lettuce Wraps with Diced Celery, Red Onion, and Fresh Herbs

Dinner: Grilled Portobello Mushrooms Stuffed with Spinach and Tomatoes

Dessert: Chilled Mixed Berry Compote with a Dollop of Fat-Free Greek Yogurt

Snack: Roasted Red Pepper and Tomato Soup

Drink: Cucumber and Mint Infused Water

Day 14:

Breakfast: Veggie-Packed Scrambled Eggs with Spinach, Mushrooms, and Tomatoes

Lunch: Roasted Vegetable Soup with Butternut Squash, Carrots, and Leeks

Dinner: Grilled Salmon with a Side of Asparagus and Cherry Tomatoes

Dessert: Grilled Peaches with a Drizzle of Balsamic Glaze

Snack: Zucchini Chips with a Sprinkle of Garlic Powder and Paprika

Drink: Iced Green Tea with Fresh Lemon Slices

Week 3
Day 15:

Breakfast: Scrambled Tofu with Spinach, Bell Peppers, and Onions

Lunch: Chickpea and Veggie Salad with Cucumber, Cherry Tomatoes, Red Onion, and Fresh Parsley

Dinner: Baked Chicken Breast with Cauliflower Mash and Steamed Green Beans

Dessert: Frozen Banana and Strawberry "Nice Cream" (blended frozen bananas and strawberries)

Snack: Spicy Roasted Chickpeas with Cumin and Paprika

Drink: Spiced Herbal Tea with Cinnamon and Ginger

Day 16:

Breakfast: Egg White Omelet with Bell Peppers, Onions, and Fresh Herbs

Lunch: Grilled Turkey Patties with Sautéed Spinach and Mushrooms

Dinner: Turkey Meatballs in a Homemade Marinara Sauce with SpaghettiSquash

Dessert: Poached Pears in Spiced Herbal Tea

Snack: Fresh Veggie Platter with Homemade Salsa or Pico de Gallo

Drink: Lemon and Lime Sparkling Water with Fresh Mint Leaves

Day 17:

Breakfast: Berry Smoothie with Unsweetened Almond Milk and a Handful of Spinach

Lunch: Grilled Eggplant and Red Pepper Stack with Fresh Herbs and a Drizzle of Balsamic Vinegar

Dinner: Grilled Tuna Steak with a Side of Roasted Zucchini and Squash

Dessert: Mixed Berry Sorbet (made with frozen berries and a splash of lemon juice)

Snack: Grilled Asparagus Spears with Lemon Zest and Sea Salt

Drink: Watermelon and Basil Infused Water

Day 18:

Breakfast: Poached Eggs over a Bed of Sautéed Kale and Cherry Tomatoes

Lunch: Spicy Black Bean Soup with Diced Tomatoes, Onions, and Cilantro

Dinner: Pan-Seared Tilapia with a Cucumber and Tomato Salad

Dessert: Baked Rhubarb with Fresh Strawberries and Vanilla Extract

Snack: Hard-Boiled Eggs with a Sprinkle of Everything Bagel Seasoning

Drink: Celery and Cucumber Juice with a Splash of Lemon

Day 19:

Breakfast: Cottage Cheese with Sliced Cucumbers and Cherry Tomatoes

Lunch: Zucchini Noodles with Tomato Basil Sauce and Grilled Chicken Strips

Dinner: Herb-Roasted Chicken Thighs with a Side of Sautéed Spinach and Garlic

Dessert: Citrus Salad with Oranges, Grapefruit, and Mint

Snack: Baked Eggplant Slices with Marinara Dipping Sauce

Drink: Pineapple and Ginger Smoothie (using water and fresh pineapple chunks)

Day 20:

Breakfast: Fresh Fruit Salad with Grapefruit, Kiwi, and Berries

Lunch: Grilled Shrimp Skewers with a Side of Roasted Asparagus and Bell Peppers

Dinner: Turkey and Cabbage Rolls with a Tomato-Based Sauce

Dessert: Grilled Pineapple Rings with a Dusting of Cinnamon

Snack: Deviled Eggs with Greek Yogurt and Mustard Filling

Drink: Herbal Iced Tea with Fresh Mint and a Hint of Stevia (optional)

Day 21:

Breakfast: Spiced Apple and Oatmeal Breakfast Bowl (using unsweetened applesauce and spices)

Lunch: Roasted Vegetable Soup with Butternut Squash, Carrots, and Leeks

Dinner: Grilled Portobello Mushrooms Stuffed with Spinach and Tomatoes

Dessert: Fresh Fruit Salad with Pineapple, Mango, and Kiwi

Snack: Fresh Veggie Spring Rolls with Lettuce, Cucumber, Carrots, and Mint (no rice paper or noodles)

Drink: Tomato and Basil Juice (fresh tomatoes blended with basil and a touch of salt)

Week 4
Day 22:

Breakfast: Cauliflower Rice Breakfast Bowl with Sautéed Vegetables and Fresh Herbs

Lunch: Grilled Chicken Salad with Mixed Greens, Cucumber, Cherry Tomatoes, and Balsamic Vinegar

Dinner: Baked Lemon Herb Chicken with Roasted Brussels Sprouts and Carrots

Dessert: Baked Cinnamon Apples with a Sprinkle of Nutmeg and Fresh Berries

Snack: Zucchini Chips with a Sprinkle of Garlic Powder and Paprika

Drink: Apple and Cinnamon Water (infuse water with apple slices and cinnamon sticks)

Day 23:

Breakfast: Baked Egg Cups with Zucchini, Red Bell Peppers, and Onions

Lunch: Tuna Salad Lettuce Wraps with Diced Celery, Red Onion, and Fresh Herbs

Dinner: Shrimp and Vegetable Stir-Fry with Bell Peppers, Snow Peas, and Ginger

Dessert: Chilled Mixed Berry Compote with a Dollop of Fat-Free Greek Yogurt

Snack: Spicy Roasted Chickpeas with Cumin and Paprika

Drink: Kale and Green Apple Smoothie (using water or unsweetened almond milk)

Day 24:

Breakfast: Greek Yogurt with Mixed Berries and a Sprinkle of Cinnamon

Lunch: Chickpea and Veggie Salad with Cucumber, Cherry Tomatoes, Red Onion, and Fresh Parsley

Dinner: Turkey Meatballs in a Homemade Marinara Sauce with Spaghetti Squash

Dessert: Frozen Banana and Strawberry "Nice Cream" (blended frozen bananas and strawberries)

Snack: Fresh Veggie Platter with Homemade Salsa or Pico de Gallo

Drink: Cucumber and Mint Infused Water

Day 25:

Breakfast: Veggie-Packed Scrambled Eggs with Spinach, Mushrooms, and Tomatoes

Lunch: Grilled Turkey Patties with Sautéed Spinach and Mushrooms

Dinner: Grilled Tuna Steak with a Side of Roasted Zucchini and Squash

Dessert: Grilled Peaches with a Drizzle of Balsamic Glaze

Snack: Baked Eggplant Slices with Marinara Dipping Sauce

Drink: Iced Green Tea with Fresh Lemon Slices

Day 26:

Breakfast: Poached Eggs over a Bed of Sautéed Kale and Cherry Tomatoes

Lunch: Spicy Black Bean Soup with Diced Tomatoes, Onions, and Cilantro

Dinner: Pan-Seared Tilapia with a Cucumber and Tomato Salad

Dessert: Poached Pears in Spiced Herbal Tea

Snack: Hard-Boiled Eggs with a Sprinkle of Everything Bagel Seasoning

Drink: Spiced Herbal Tea with Cinnamon and Ginger

Day 27:

Breakfast: Scrambled Tofu with Spinach, Bell Peppers, and Onions

Lunch: Zucchini Noodles with Tomato Basil Sauce and Grilled Chicken Strips

Dinner: Herb-Roasted Chicken Thighs with a Side of Sautéed Spinach and Garlic

Dessert: Mixed Berry Sorbet (made with frozen berries and a splash of lemon juice)

Snack: Fresh Veggie Spring Rolls with Lettuce, Cucumber, Carrots, and Mint (no rice paper or noodles)

Drink: Lemon and Lime Sparkling Water with Fresh Mint Leaves

Day 28:

Breakfast: Baked Tomato and Egg Cups with Fresh Basil and Oregano

Lunch: Grilled Eggplant and Red Pepper Stack with Fresh Herbs and a Drizzle of Balsamic Vinegar

Dinner: Turkey and Cabbage Rolls with a Tomato-Based Sauce

Dessert: Grilled Pineapple Rings with a Dusting of Cinnamon

Snack: Grilled Asparagus Spears with Lemon Zest and Sea Salt

Drink: Watermelon and Basil Infused Water

Day 29:

Breakfast: Berry Smoothie with Unsweetened Almond Milk and a Handful of Spinach

Lunch: Tuna Salad Lettuce Wraps with Diced Celery, Red Onion, and Fresh Herbs

Dinner: Grilled Salmon with a Side of Asparagus and Cherry Tomatoes

Dessert: Baked Rhubarb with Fresh Strawberries and Vanilla Extract

Snack: Deviled Eggs with Greek Yogurt and Mustard Filling

Drink: Celery and Cucumber Juice with a Splash of Lemon

Day 30:

Breakfast: Fresh Fruit Salad with Grapefruit, Kiwi, and Berries

Lunch: Roasted Vegetable Soup with Butternut Squash, Carrots, and Leeks

Dinner: Baked Lemon Herb Chicken with Roasted Brussels Sprouts and Carrots

Dessert: Frozen Banana and Strawberry "Nice Cream" (blended frozen bananas and strawberries)

Snack: Cucumber Slices with Tuna Salad Topping (made with tuna, celery, and Greek yogurt)

Drink: Kale and Green Apple Smoothie (using water or unsweetened almond milk)

This 30-day plan provides a balanced mix of meals, snacks, desserts, and drinks, ensuring that each day is filled with variety while sticking to the zero-point guidelines. The plan supports weight loss goals by focusing on nutrient-rich, low-calorie foods that keep you satisfied throughout the day.

Conclusion

Congratulations on reaching the end of the No-Point Weight Loss Cookbook! By now, you've explored a wide array of delicious, satisfying recipes that not only support your weight loss goals but also nourish your body with wholesome, nutrient-dense foods.

Throughout this journey, you've discovered that eating well doesn't have to mean counting every calorie or limiting yourself to tiny portions. Instead, you've embraced a flexible and sustainable approach to weight loss, one that allows you to enjoy your food while making healthier choices every day. The recipes in this cookbook are designed to be more than just a temporary diet—they're a gateway to a lifelong commitment to better health.

As you continue on your path to a healthier lifestyle, remember that the key to lasting success is balance and enjoyment. These no-point recipes are here to support you in maintaining that balance, offering meals that are easy to prepare, full of flavor, and completely satisfying. Whether you're cooking for yourself or sharing meals with loved ones, you now have a versatile toolkit of recipes that can fit seamlessly into any day, any occasion.

Most importantly, this cookbook is a reminder that healthy eating can and should be enjoyable. By focusing on foods that naturally fuel your body and keep you satisfied, you're not just losing weight—you're creating a positive, sustainable relationship with food that will benefit you for years to come.

Thank you for choosing the No-Point Weight Loss Cookbook as your companion on this journey. Here's to your continued success, happiness, and health—one delicious meal at a time!

Recipes Index

Roasted Vegetable Soup with Butternut Squash, Carrots, and Leeks   30

Scrambled Tofu with Spinach, Bell Peppers, and Onions 19

Shrimp and Vegetable Stir-Fry with Bell Peppers, Snow Peas, and Ginger   38

Slow-Cooked Beef Stew with Carrots, Celery, and Onions   48

Spaghetti Squash with Marinara Sauce and Sautéed Vegetables (Zucchini, Mushrooms, and Spinach)   26

Spiced Apple and Oatmeal Breakfast Bowl (using unsweetened applesauce and spices)   16

Spiced Herbal Tea with Cinnamon and Ginger   72

Spicy Black Bean Soup with Diced Tomatoes, Onions, and Cilantro   35

Spicy Roasted Chickpeas with Cumin and Paprika   64

Stuffed Bell Peppers with Ground Turkey and Diced Vegetables 44

Tomato and Basil Juice 78

Tuna Salad Lettuce Wraps with Diced Celery, Red Onion, and Fresh Herbs   27

Turkey and Cabbage Rolls with a Tomato-Based Sauce 46

Turkey and Cabbage Stir-Fry with Ginger and Garlic   29

Turkey Meatballs in a Homemade Marinara Sauce with Spaghetti Squash40

Veggie-Packed Scrambled Eggs with Spinach, Mushrooms, and Tomatoes   13

Watermelon and Basil Infused Water   74

Zucchini Chips with a Sprinkle of Garlic Powder and Paprika   63

Zucchini Noodles with Tomato Basil Sauce and Grilled Chicken Strips   34

**Dear Reader, wait, just before you go,
Did you enjoy reading this book?**

PLEASE CAN YOU CONSIDER LEAVING US YOUR FEEDBACK?

Your feedback is incredibly important to me and helps other readers discover my work. If you enjoyed the book and you have 60 seconds, it would mean a lot to me if you could leave a quick review on Amazon.

It's good for the book and I'd love to know how you benefited from it. I really appreciate you taking the time to read this book. This means a lot to me, I do not take it for granted.

**Here's how you can do it:
Click on the book's title to go to its detailed page.
Scroll down until you find the "Customer Reviews" section.**

**You'll see a button that says "Write a customer review." Click on it.
You'll be asked to give the book a star rating from 1 to 5 stars. Give your honest rating
Share your thoughts about the book. What did you enjoy? What stood out to you? Your honest feedback is appreciated!**

**After writing your review, click the "Submit" button.
Your review will be posted on the book's Amazon page and will help other readers make an informed decision.
Thank you so much for your support!**

**THANK YOU!
Best regards,
Jenkins.**

THE COMPLETE NO POINT WEIGHT LOSS COOKBOOK

Satisfying Recipes That Keep You Full and Slim Without Counting Calories with 30-Day Meal Plan

Dr. Rachel Jenkins

Made in United States
Troutdale, OR
10/04/2024

23429786R00053